Certificate of Proficiency English Practice

Certificate of Proficiency English Practice

Ona Low

 Edward Arnold

First published 1979
by Edward Arnold (Publishers) Ltd
41 Bedford Square, London WC1B 3DQ

British Library Cataloguing in Publication Data

Low, Ona
  Certificate of Proficiency English practice.
  1. English language—Text-books for foreigners
  2. English language—Composition and exercises
  I. Title
  428′.2′4   PE1128

  ISBN 0–7131 8006–4

By the same author:
Certificate of Proficiency English Practice KEY
First Certificate in English Course, and KEY
A New Certificate of Proficiency English, and KEY
First Certificate in English Practice, and KEY
Speak English Fluently: Book 1
Speak English Fluently: Book 2

Text set in 11/12 pt Photon Times, printed and bound
in Great Britain at The Pitman Press, Bath

Preface

As in the case of 'First Certificate in English Practice', the 'Certificate of Proficiency Practice' is intended primarily to supplement an existing course book, in this instance the 'Certificate of Proficiency English Course'. The latter is concerned mainly with providing a comprehensive course in English as a Foreign Language at an advanced level, and as such, introduces very considerable general language learning material. This material may be of use not only to the Certificate of Proficiency examination candidate, but also to all learners who wish to achieve near-native language facility, together with the ability to express themselves on many subjects and in many forms. The present Practice book is closely related to the examination, and should assist students to make the most effective use of their knowledge and skill in answering questions. Much valuable advice is given on how to tackle each part of the examination.

When class meetings are restricted to a maximum of 4–6 hours a week for no more than one session, the teacher may prefer to concentrate on the Practice book, especially if the students have already reached the standard of language proficiency required for the examination. In this case, the 'Certificate of Proficiency in English Course' may serve as a useful reference book.

One of the main difficulties experienced by the teacher of a Proficiency class is a possible lack of graded material for the students. Many students join a Proficiency class after passing the First Certificate with the over-optimistic ambition of preparing in a single year for an examination which would be a challenge even for University students of English in most countries. They may be immediately confronted with material of examination level and inevitably feel bewildered and discouraged by its difficulty.

The material in this book is presented in three stages. The first of these is intended for students who have either passed the First Certificate or have completed a six-to-seven-year reasonably intensive school English course. The second is at an intermediate stage, and the third consists of two sets of model question papers designed to give practice in tackling the examination effectively and in timing answers. Despite this grading, however, standards throughout are high and teachers need to advise students about the very considerable home study and supplementary reading essential in preparing for the examination. This is especially important if the student (who may have only a limited time to spend in Britain or for regular class attendance) attempts the Herculean task of achieving examination level in one year.

A Key is published separately and this includes Listening Comprehension passages. The questions on these passages are in this book.

Contents

Stage 1: Post First Certificate

Stage 2: Intermediate Level

Stage 3: Examination Level

Arrangement

The material is grouped in three stages. In the first two of these, graded in difficulty for students in the early and middle stages of a Proficiency course, two or three examples of each of the various types of question are grouped together; it is left to the teacher, or to the student working alone, to select items for practice according to the time available and special needs and interests.

At these two levels the emphasis is on learning as well as practice. Accordingly, the material presented is intended to promote:

(a) the enrichment of vocabulary and familiarisation with more advanced structures
(b) training in advanced reading: that is to say, reading with full comprehension without necessarily knowing the meaning of each individual word
(c) concentrated reading and listening
(d) understanding, and expressing information gained from such understanding
(e) the development of a near-native feeling for language

Comprehension passages may therefore be slightly longer than those on examination papers and there may be more questions relating to them. Interview material is similar to that featured in the examination but progresses in difficulty.

The third stage consists of two groups of model examination papers. Each paper corresponds as nearly as possible to an actual paper and students are recommended to deal with each paper as a whole under examination conditions, especially with regard to the *time* taken for completion. British pupils are trained in school to deal with examination questions briskly, and in what may seem an extremely short time as compared with the five or six hours available for writing in some other countries. Experience in timing is therefore important, as well as practice in the techniques necessary for achieving a satisfactory standard.

In the first stage, the author gives detailed advice and guidance on the most effective way of tackling examination questions. This advice appears before the exercises on each paper.

Also in the first stage, model answers to some kinds of questions are included to indicate the kind of answers looked for by the examiner. In this case the passages themselves may be slightly more difficult than the following ones for student practice. An example of a model answer to the Paper 1 comprehension passage appears at each of the three stages as, owing to its unfamiliarity, many students find this question particularly difficult. Until the present time, passages of this kind that have appeared on papers have been characterised by a somewhat similar theme and treatment, although the syllabus does admit a wide range of subject and approach. Several of the passages introduced here, therefore, do not conform to the type so far utilised, but offer practice in dealing with other forms of writing.

Stage 1
Post First Certificate

1 Composition

Section A: Composition Writing Suggestions and advice

Nature of this test

Two compositions are required. One of these may be of a descriptive or narrative type; the other will involve possibly a general survey of a subject or the expression of opinions. The latter may be one-sided, or arguments for and against a certain point of view, or advantages and drawbacks of a suggestion or situation.

Candidates are advised to spend an equal time on each of these two compositions and on Section B of the paper, that is to say, one hour on each.

Examiner's assessment

In determining the mark to be earned by a composition, the examiner is likely to consider the following:

Ideas expressed
No reference is made in the examination syllabus to the actual material of the composition, beyond the need for relevancy (the fact that it deals with the subject set). Creativity and imagination, even an interest in current ideas and considered judgment about them, are not necessarily related to language ability. However an ability to express ideas is of little value without some ideas to express.

Above all the composition must deal with the subject set: the nature of this must have been fully understood, and all the ideas introduced must be closely related to it.

Construction
The syllabus refers to the importance of relevance and organisation in the composition as a whole, and, where appropriate, of the individual paragraphs. A well-organised composition will have the following features:
  (*a*) evidence of careful preparation and planning of the material before the writing
  (*b*) a satisfactory beginning and ending
  (*c*) a logical and natural development of the theme, the attention given to each

topic related to its importance and relevance in the general scheme

(*d*) the extension of each topic into a satisfactorily constructed paragraph.

Language and expression

These are referred to in the syllabus as:

'the quality of the language employed: the range and appropriateness of vocabulary and sentence structure'.

The marking of a composition is more of a positive than a negative process. That is to say, although marks will certainly be brought down by errors, they will equally certainly be raised for fluency and range of expresson, which show that a candidate has an extensive vocabulary and control over sentence structure.

Absence of mistakes

The syllabus refers to:

'the correctness of grammatical construction, punctuation and spelling'.

Preparing and writing a composition

The material

While some people undoubtedly have more imagination and creative skill than others, the ability to produce individual and relevant ideas is largely a matter of training, and can be cultivated in the following ways:

(*a*) Not only reading, but considering what is being read: are the ideas expressed practical, reasonable, consistent? How far do they differ from your own viewpoint? The same may be applied to ideas heard on radio and television.

(*b*) Speculation about people and their behaviour, current conventions, accepted beliefs and assumptions, fashionable theories and attitudes, and the immense variety of situations in everyday life. This involves the cultivation of curiosity, detachment and a wide interest in one's surroundings.

(*c*) Discussion with acquaintances.

(*d*) A consideration of all the composition topics suggested in this book, not necessarily with the intention of writing about them but merely to speculate about what could be written.

The examination composition

(*a*) Only two hours are available for writing the two compositions, so it is important to waste as little time as possible on choosing which to attempt. One of the subjects may appear a challenging and interesting one, and you know you could write about it excellently in your own language. Make sure, however, that your ability in English, especially the range of your vocabulary, is sufficient to do justice to it now. A less interesting subject that is more within your range, and if presented *effectively* will probably earn better marks, may be advisable. Having chosen your first subject and set to work preparing it, avoid waste of time (and confidence) by changing your mind about it. In other words, make a firm and sensible decision in the minimum amount of time.

Some people find it useful to choose the second subject at the same time as the first and to collect a few ideas about it before starting to write the first composition. When they return to these ideas, they often find that others have come into their mind in the interval, often more interesting ones than those noted, and the preparation goes far more smoothly as a result.

(b) Read the subjects set with concentration, making absolutely certain you understand what is required; do not misinterpret the subject and write an inappropriate essay.

(c) With practice you will find that it seems natural from the start to consider the subject under four or five headings, which will themselves form the plan. Otherwise jot (write) down any ideas that come into your head. Continue until you can think of no more and then set those you have into some order, discarding any that have little relation to the subject.

(d) Check again that you are interpreting the subject set appropriately.

Arranging the composition

It is always advisable to construct a plan which shows the topic of each paragraph and possibly a few ideas to be developed. Here is an example of a plan:

Subject

Transport developments during the past two centuries have enabled far more people than ever before in history to move to or visit other places and other countries. To what extent do you consider that this increased mobility has affected people's lives and outlooks?

Plan

1 Introduction: the stationary existence of most people up to two centuries ago and its effect on their lives and interests.

2 Some effects of mobility on living standards and opportunities: career possibilities depending on job changes, and study possibilities.

3 Leisure-time enjoyment: holidays, Sunday outings, keeping in touch with relatives, hobbies, sport.

4 Superficial influence: something to talk about and add interest to news about those places, possibly new friends made, a few ideas (e.g. food) adopted.

5 Most people probably not much influenced by travel: impressions of other places and new ideas about life and living derived rather from mass media and advertising.

6 Travel and possibly work abroad has influenced minority: adventure, challenge, tolerance, adaptability, greater understanding of other people and the world in general.

It would be easy to misinterpret this subject and to extend it to cover international business and trade, which have obviously had far wider effects. Visiting or moving to other places and countries, however, was the subject of the question.

The opening and closing paragraphs have their own importance. The opening paragraph, especially the first sentence, is very important as this is the first impression of your writing that the reader gets, and it will influence his judgment. It should aim to awaken immediate interest, besides, naturally, serving to introduce the main theme of the composition. Among the various approaches to an opening paragraph are the following possibilities:
- (*a*) Background information influencing the later expression of an opinion.
- (*b*) Either a direct quotation or reference to a proverb, saying or other relevant statement.
- (*c*) A challenging or surprising statement.
- (*d*) An anecdote or example leading to the first main topic.
- (*e*) An idea that will serve as a contrast to what follows.
- (*f*) A questioning reference to the idea expressed in the question.

The final paragraph should bring the composition to an appropriate conclusion, leaving at the same time, if appropriate, a pleasing impression of the writer's personality, humour or intelligent interest in his subject. These are a few of the many possibilities:
- (*a*) The application of what has been said to the future or to some other field.
- (*b*) An unexpected apparent contradiction to what has been expressed, which leaves the reader wondering.
- (*c*) An anecdote or other reference illustrating what has been argued.
- (*d*) A quotation.
- (*e*) A topic related to the one developed in the opening paragraph, which brings the composition full circle.
- (*f*) A statement, challenge, question that will leave the reader thinking.

Between a fifth and a quarter of the time available for answering the question should be devoted to gathering material and arranging it. With most of the creative, original and concentrated thinking completed, you can now give the whole of your attention to expressing the ideas in the best possible way.

Writing the composition
- (*a*) *Above all, avoid thinking in your own language and translating.* Doing this inevitably leads to 'interference mistakes', and to the kind of expression which might sound natural in your language but would appear false and clumsy in English.
- (*b*) Make full use of the vocabulary you know, remembering however that the long, impressive-sounding word is often not the most suitable. The language you use must obviously be adapted to the material and the way in which it is presented: formal, literary, sensational, colloquial or otherwise.

Unless there is some purpose in using it, slang is best avoided, and the more striking idioms introduced only when they really fit the case, not just to show off your knowledge of them.

Conversational and other verbal abbreviations are not normally used in a formal composition: their main purpose in writing is to give the impression that the writer is chatting casually to the reader.

(c) Sentence length and construction should show variety and be adapted to the idea expressed. Avoid overusing the long involved sentence even if you can control it effectively.

Variety in construction applies also to word and clause order, besides the grammatical pattern of the sentence.

(d) Paragraph construction is one aspect of the overall arrangement. The topic being developed should be clear and it will be extended in a variety of ways, including illustration, substantiation (providing evidence) and the filling in of details.

Reading through

Ideally each sentence should be re-read on completion, but this may slow down and even obstruct the flow of ideas.

However, try to read each paragraph on completion, and above all, read the whole composition slowly and extremely critically when it is finished.

Check not only the spelling, punctuation, grammar (including verb tenses), word order and sentence construction, but also whether the ideas are logically set out and make sense. You may want to make some improvements, such as replacing certain words by more appropriate ones, but do not overdo this. It may take more time than you can spare, and the final result of too much 'improvement' may be less satisfactory than you hoped—and harder to read, as well!

Avoid writing the whole essay in rough first and then copying it hurriedly in the last few moments available, possibly without enough time to finish it. You may, however, wish to prepare particularly difficult short sections in this way.

Subjects for Composition

Narrative

1 Relate your experience of a holiday during which everything proved to be different from what the travel agent arranging it had told you.

2 When turning out a cupboard, you find three contrasting objects, each of which recalls an episode in your earlier life. Narrate each episode, relating it to the object which recalls it.

3 You have always been terrified of flying, but circumstances force you to make a journey by air. Explain the circumstances and describe your feelings before

and during the flight, which, although relatively uneventful, does not change your attitude in any way.

4 In the district where you live there have been floods which have caused a good deal of destruction and many problems for human beings. Write the article about the situation which a journalist who had toured the area might submit to a local newspaper.

Description

1 Five minutes' wait at a bus stop. Describe your surroundings, what is going on around you, and your feelings and thoughts as they change during the time of waiting. These may include plans, memories, hopes and worries. There will probably be some association between your thoughts and what you see around you.

2 You live in a block of flats. Each of your neighbours, above, below, and on either side of you is something of a nuisance and makes life unpleasant for you in a different way. Describe the people involved and the various ways in which they annoy you.

3 Describe a town in your country which is very attractive to foreign tourists, giving some of its historical or other background and explaining why tourists appreciate it.

4 Your ideal home—its position and surroundings, appearance, amenities and special appeal.

5 Your flat on the seventh floor faces east and west, with contrasting views in each direction. Describe one of these views as it appears at a certain time of the day, the other as it appears by moonlight or by street lighting.

Fact and opinion

1 You have to give a radio talk in which you will try to persuade listeners to make use of public transport whenever possible rather than use their own private cars. Write the script you will read from.

2 In some parts of the world a young married couple form part of an extended family system: they live with, or very close to, a number of the relations of the husband or wife, including parents, brothers and sisters, and possibly other relations too. Discuss some of the benefits the couple may enjoy and also some of the drawbacks of living in this way.

3 A younger person than yourself, for whose welfare you feel in some way responsible, is considering taking up a career you know something about, and has written to you for your advice. Write a reply in which you set out what you regard as the overall advantages of this type of work, but also suggesting why the choice may not be an ideal one for the person concerned.

4 The advantages of having variable weather.

5 How would you explain the fact that an increasing number of marriages end in divorce?

6   What is your opinion of the importance of sport in the present-day world?
7   To what extent do you consider there should be a difference between the up-
    bringing and education of boys and girls?
8   What contribution can people over the age of sixty make to society?

Section B: Comprehension
Suggestions and advice

Nature of this test

The examination syllabus refers to:
> 'questions on one or more passages, designed to test comprehension and
> perception of the effective use of English'.

A more detailed explanation is given in the Syllabus Notes on the papers:
> 'this section is intended to test both the candidate's comprehension of the
> passage and his perception of the writer's technique: of the way, for example, in
> which he uses particular words to produce particular effects and the way in
> which he organises his material'.

Many candidates find this a particularly difficult question as it calls for an ability
to interpret, criticise and evaluate qualities of arrangement and word usage. They
may be able to recognise such features easily in their own language, but not in a
foreign one.

Questions on the passage normally average between 7–9 in number and may be
concerned with any of the following features.

Content and presentation of ideas

(*a*) General comprehension.

(*b*) The writer's treatment of certain ideas: e.g. critically, approvingly,
     mockingly, humorously, with fantasy.

(*c*) How certain effects are created e.g. effects of humour, absurdity, dignity,
     mystery, fear, shock, irritation, exaggeration.

(*d*) The choice and/or emphasis of certain details to intensify the impression of
     a person or place.

(*e*) The means used to capture the reader's attention or engage his sympathy.

(*f*) The use of *implication*—that is to say, the use of ideas and words which,
     besides their obvious meaning, suggest additional meanings and feelings
     that the reader becomes aware of rather than registers consciously.

Arrangement of ideas

(*a*) The connection or contrast between various parts of the passage.

(*b*) The effectiveness of the beginning or ending, or of the introduction of an

9

idea or expression at a certain point in the passage.

(*c*) The order in which the ideas are presented, especially when this is unusual: the effects achieved by the way in which ideas are developed.

Stylistic features

The achievement of certain effects:

(*a*) how a word or word group can achieve a certain effect or convey an impression of a person or scene.

(*b*) how characters are revealed by their conversation and general manner of speaking.

(*c*) the use of repetition.

The choice and use of words and word groups:

(*a*) The quotation of a word or word group which serves a certain purpose e.g. illustration, expansion or definition of an earlier expression.

(*b*) The special appropriateness of a certain word or word group possibly in comparison with a less appropriate means of expression.

(*c*) The suitability and/or significance of metaphorical words and phrases.

(*d*) Where a word should be emphasised or the reason for implied emphasis.

(*e*) Reasons for certain stylistic and related features such as direct speech, other quotation marks, italics, capital letters, foreign expressions.

(*f*) Explanation of certain grammatical features: e.g. reasons for pronoun changes, unexpected subject/verb agreement, choice of conjunction. Questions on the Paper 3 comprehension passage may demand pronoun or other identification: in Paper 1, the *reason* for the use of one form and not another may be asked.

Guidelines

1 About one hour is available for this section. The time needed to deal with each part will vary considerably, but if 8 questions are set, the average time that can be spent on each (allowing ten minutes for reading the passage and five for reading through the answers) is $5\frac{1}{2}$ minutes. This will include time for the careful consideration of ideas, expressing them suitably and possibly having to rephrase or correct your answer.

Your answers will therefore be *concise*—as short as you can make them while expressing the ideas adequately. The model answers in this book should give some idea of normal (and in some cases maximum) length that there is time for. This ability to compress and write relevantly will need considerable pre-examination practice.

2 Having read the passage carefully (twice if necessary), study each question with concentration, so that you thoroughly understand what kind of answer is required. A hazy idea of the question will result in the wrong kind of answer and loss of marks.

Decide which of the following is required:

10

(a) general comprehension of ideas,

(b) a consideration of the impression the writer is trying to give,

(c) the writer's skill in interesting his reader,

(d) the effectiveness of the writer's arrangement of his material,

(e) the effects created by particular words, or the reasons for his choice of one word rather than another.

3   Here are a few suggestions for dealing with certain types of question:

(a) Effects of humour, irritation, fear, exaggeration etc. These may depend on the details included, words used (possibly their actual sound), exclamations and sentence length.

(b) Means of capturing the reader's attention: surprise or shock? apparent absurdity? humour? a suggestion that something important or extremely interesting is about to follow?

(c) Similarity or contrast between parts of the passage—often the beginning and ending. Such contrasts may apply to changed feelings or ideas, words and sentence structures, an appeal to the reader's attention—consider exactly what devices in fact cause the likeness or contrast.

(d) Order of ideas. This may seem unnatural: try to appreciate what an unexpected arrangement of ideas may be intended to convey.

(e) Stylistic effects. These can be of various kinds and can include conversation as it reveals a character (ideas expressed and words and sentence structures used e.g. formal and dignified, disjointed and almost meaningless, aggressive); also words and phrases chosen for their effect.

Examples:

(i) What usually 'perches' (line 30) and how can this idea be applied to Totnes Castle?
(See page 14, question *j*)

(ii) Quote three expressions from the third paragraph with which the writer gives a clear idea of the aggressiveness of perambulators and their occupants.
(See page 87, question *c*)

(iii) Why should the sun 'draw himself from the water' (line 18) and not just 'rise'?
(See page 139, question *f*)

General advice

Make sure you examine the point referred to in the passage for evidence on which to base your answer.

The foregoing recommendations show something of the complexity of answers to questions on this type of passage, and may indicate the general method of approach; this is to analyse the ideas and words of the passage to explain the secrets of the writer's technique.

You are recommended to study the three model passages and answers in this book (pages 12–14, 86–88, and 137–139), apply the foregoing advice to them, and then work on other passages.

Passages for Comprehension

Read the following passages and then answer the questions which follow them.

Model questions and answers

The effect of neatness and completeness is helped by the setting. Totnes is surrounded by plump hills, all fat with grass and neatly ribbed along the contours by the walks which centuries of ambling sheep and cattle have created. When the sun catches these walks just right, it makes the hillside look like rich
5 green corduroy, in perfect contrast to the cattle themselves: as red as the Devon soil. Every time I paused to lean on a gate, one or two of them hurried towards me with that curious impression of urgency which cattle can generate, and which always fades to caution over the last few yards until they come to a halt, blinking and swishing their tails and looking as if they have
10 forgotten what it was they intended to tell me.

Far away, beyond and behind this agricultural plenty, is Dartmoor. It lies on the horizon, a slightly sinister silhouette in grey, managing to look flattened out yet high up at one and the same time: a reminder that Totnes is lucky to be so comfortable just as the seagulls are a reminder that Totnes was
15 originally founded by mariners. Or so they say. Geoffrey of Monmouth is supposed to be the authority for this, but then he wrote history in a highly imaginative way.

According to Geoffrey, Brutus the Trojan was wanted by the police in connection with some unpleasantness in the Mediterranean, so he made himself
20 scarce and—for no particular reason—landed in South Devon, on Totnes shore. Geoffrey of Monmouth had evidence to prove it: the Brutus Stone, the boulder Brutus set foot on when he got out of his boat. You can see it for yourself today, halfway up Fore Street; which means either that the level of the river Dart has gone down a couple of hundred feet or that Brutus the
25 Trojan had an impressive stride.

The Normans built the castle, but it had a very placid history: even in the Wars of the Roses, even in the Civil War, Totnes managed to stay out of harm's way. Which is probably why the castle is in such amazingly good condition: a beautifully simple circular stone wall, 70 or 80 feet in diameter,
30 perched high on a mound with a ditch at the bottom. The crenellations are bold, with plenty of arrow-slits, and when you look up at the castle from the town below, it looks surprisingly like the sort of crown Laurence Olivier wore

in the film of Henry V: really just a simple headband with a cut-out pattern running around the top. This resemblance gave me a sudden thought: could it
35 be that royal crowns were originally modelled on the basic shape of a castle? After all, they were both symbols of authority: one reason why castles look so impressive is that they were intended to impress. The discontented peasant who came out of his hovel feeling like taking industrial action took one look up the hill and changed his mind.
40   While I was having this insight, I caught a powerful whiff of garlic—wild garlic. The slopes around the castle were thick with it. Which made me wonder whether the Normans brought it over with them, or if it was native to England; or maybe the Normans planted great beds of the stuff around their castles as an asset for the cookhouse combined with a stage-one defence
45 against any possible unwelcome visitors . . . I shall never know because, at that point, further thought was rendered impossible by the tuneless electronic bray of the ice-cream van. Not even Totnes can escape this peculiarly British form of pollution.

(a) In what way can the reader tell from the first sentence that this is an extract from a longer passage?

The first six words clearly refer back to a statement about Totnes itself and the writer is now going to describe the town's setting.

(b) Quote a phrase from the passage which justifies the description of the hillside as looking 'like rich green corduroy' (l. 4–5).

all fat with grass and ribbed along the contours

(c) Justify the writer's description of the hillside as 'in perfect contrast to the cattle' (l. 5).

The hillside is a rich green while the cattle are a rich red—two complementary colours.

(d) What effect is given by the reference to the cows 'swishing' their tails rather than just 'moving' them? (l.9).

'Swishing' is a very decided sideways movement, conveying the sound of movement through air.

(e) Suggest briefly two details in the first paragraph which the writer refers back to with the words 'this agricultural plenty' at the beginning of the second paragraph.

These are the plump hills all fat with grass, and the cattle.

(f) Why should the writer describe Dartmoor as 'a slightly sinister silhouette' (l. 12)?

Dartmoor is represented as a remote high grey mass against the sky. It appears a little frightening and in obvious contrast to the sunny rich

13

green pastures near at hand.

(g) How does the final statement in paragraph two, 'he wrote history in a highly imaginative way', relate to the information about Brutus given in the following paragraph?

It suggests that the information may be merely the fruit of Geoffrey's imagination and therefore untrue.

(h) Comment on the writer's treatment of the Brutus legend in lines 18–21.

He provides a humorous effect by telling his story in contemporary terms as if he were reporting an event in a popular newspaper or detective novel.

(i) What two features of the third paragraph suggest that the writer is to some extent making fun of the story of Brutus the Trojan?

He applies modern ideas of the police and crime to a story of the ancient world. He makes fun of the legend of the Brutus Stone by exposing the highly improbable nature of the tradition attached to it.

(j) What usually 'perches' (l. 30) and how can this idea be applied to Totnes Castle?

A bird perches or stands in a high position and this idea applies to the castle, which stands high on a mound.

(k) What modern practice is the writer referring to in the words 'taking industrial action' (l. 38) and what form might this have taken in the case of a medieval peasant?

Present-day workers 'take industrial action' when they go on strike against their bosses. The peasants might have organised some kind of rebellion against their master, the occupier of the castle, or merely refused to work.

(l) What two features of garlic are being referred to in the phrases 'an asset to the cookhouse' (l. 44) and 'a stage one defence against any possible unwelcome visitors' (l. 44–45)?

Garlic can be used as a flavouring in cooking. Its smell is strong and unpleasant so it might have repelled anyone climbing the mound to attack the castle before he could even reach it.

(m) Why does the writer regard the ice-cream van referred to in lines 47–48 as a 'form of pollution'?

The noise of its chimes destroys and thus 'pollutes' the quietness.

First passage

The dew was still on the ground as we took our bicycles out of the shed at the bottom of the yard. I took the small-wheeled Moulton, my husband the old roadster we'd picked up in a market, which was so heavy we were convinced it was all iron.

5   Sharp lemon sunlight slanted down on to the moss-covered roofs and flint walls of the surrounding cottages. It was Sunday: our neighbours' curtains were still drawn. Tiptoeing out into the lane, we mounted and pedalled along the silent village street, out into the pale gold of the countryside.

    The air was so fresh and clear it bit into the nostrils and the back of the
10 throat. Immediately I became aware of the smells, bringing those Proustian moments of total recall that have no part in car-travel—the smell of manure from a farmyard, leaves, sudden sharp scents from the hedges.

    We took the road to Thurning. Norfolk is flat but not, like Lincolnshire or the Fens, without rises or falls of any kind. On a heavy, old-fashioned bike,
15 the least little dip can assume an alarming significance; but now we were fresh and, exhilarated by our freedom and the glory of the day, we sped along between beech hedges, rusting with the turning year, by small streams, beside fields of brilliant green.

    Our passing made almost no sound, just the gentle tick-tick-tick of coasting
20 wheels, the occasional tinny clank of a mudguard, our own breathing as we pedalled up an incline in the dizzying air. In the silence we could hear the song of a robin, the rustle of small creatures in the hedges. Living in London, I had forgotten silence. In the city night it may sometimes be quiet, but it is a dead quiet. In the country the silence has life.

25   We met no cars—only the vicar on his bike, speeding downhill towards us with his cassock flying like the wings of a great black bird, on his way to take a service in an outlying church. We raised our hands to each other in the country way.

    By now we were beginning to feel that persistent ache at the top of the legs
30 that goes away immediately one dismounts, but comes back again with pedalling. So we staggered into a village pub, and drank a pint of cider each and talked to a man with a soulful-eyed honey-cream labrador which came and begged for crisps. 'She's too human,' he said sadly, pulling the dog's ears. 'She takes things too much to heart, like.' After that we ate our sandwiches on
35 the Coronation seat and then we mounted our bikes, a little more slowly than before, and pedalled on.

    This unimpeded cycling through the countryside was beginning to intoxicate us: no public transport to depend on, no traffic jams, no possibilities of breakdown or fuel-shortage—just our own leg-power. We felt we could go
40 anywhere. Should we make a detour to Blickling Hall? Or to Salle to see the church again? Even Norwich seemed a possibility. But seeing that the sun

was getting low, we acknowledged our limitations at last and set off back towards home.

As we pedalled on through the villages there was a smell of wood smoke
45 now and lights were appearing in the windows. Evening mists were beginning to rise. At last we came to a familiar landmark—a little railway house at the end of a disused line, its diamond-paned windows lit up like jewels, a reminder of the time when it was easier to get about the countryside than it is now.

(a) What impression do the first seven words of the passage create that would not be conveyed by the words 'It was still very early'?

(b) How is the impression of early morning increased by the use of the word 'slanted' (l.5) as applied to the sunlight?

(c) Quote two other phrases from the second paragraph that suggest an early hour in the day.

(d) What quality of the air is conveyed by the word 'bit' in line 9?

(e) What single word in the fourth paragraph reveals that the outing took place in the autumn?

(f) Why are the words used in line 19 to convey the bicycle noises specially effective?

(g) Explain the difference between the town's 'dead quiet' in lines 23–24, and the country's 'silence that has life' in line 24.

(h) Explain why the pronoun 'we' in line 29 is replaced by 'one' in line 30.

(i) Explain how the word 'staggered' (l.31) rather than 'walked' relates to what has preceded it.

(j) Quote the words in the eighth paragraph that most nearly relate to 'unimpeded' in line 37.

(k) In what ways are the ideas presented in the first two paragraphs and in the final one in direct contrast?

Second passage

The railway station at Arkenshaw is not at the best of times a noticeably cheerful place. In the dusk of that October day it was as though the train had drawn into a cavern. Antony Maitland followed the porter who was carrying his suitcase down the platform, and scanned the group of people who were
5 waiting beyond the barrier for a first sight of Chris Conway, his instructing solicitor, who was punctilious in the matter of meeting trains even though Maitland's destination was only the Midland Hotel next door. And there Chris was, not looking very different from the first time they had met five years ago; a man of medium height, in his early thirties now, with rather un-
10 ruly brown hair that had probably been red when he was younger. The slightly worried look was natural to him, and didn't necessarily mean trouble. Anyway, he brightened a little when he saw Antony approaching.

The car, also as usual, was parked illegally in what should have been a stand for taxis only. Chris directed the disposal of Antony's suitcase in the
15 boot and climbed into the driver's seat only a moment after his passenger had

16

installed himself. 'I'm taking you home for dinner,' he said, 'if that's all right with you.'

'Much more agreeable than the hotel restaurant,' said Maitland with satisfaction.

20 They turned right out of the station into Swinegate and passed the Midland Hotel leaving behind them the four lightly-draped nymphs who guard the fountain in the centre of the square, and now Chris was trying to edge the car into the centre lane. 'Not much further now,' he went on, but whether he was encouraging his passenger or himself wasn't clear. 'You can say this much
25 about Ingleton Crescent, it's pretty central.'

'You can say more for it than that, I should have thought,' said Antony, eyeing the passing scene tranquilly. From here in the heart of the town you couldn't see Comstock's Mill, which loomed over it like a benevolent ogre, at once offending the eye and satisfying the needs of a large part of the popula-
30 tion for gainful employment, nor could you see the dark hills beyond the town. Only the smoke-grimed buildings had any reality, the shop windows brightly lighted, the double-decker bus that was barring their way. And at the sight of this last Maitland sat suddenly bolt upright and said, 'Heaven and earth!' in an awed tone. Chris jumped, gripped the steering wheel more tight-
35 ly, and said, 'Don't *do* that!' in a peevish tone.

'But you should have warned me. You've done away with the trams.'

'It wasn't a personal decision.' Conway had got over his fright and was amused again. 'As a matter of fact, I think it was a silly idea, because the
40 buses take up just as much room and are smelly into the bargain.'

'That's progress for you,' Maitland sympathised. They were well into the centre lane now, which was just as well, because the traffic lights were coming up where he knew they had to turn. 'I must say, it doesn't seem like Arkenshaw without them though.'

(a) Explain why the writer describes Arkenshaw Station as a 'cavern' (l. 3) on the occasion referred to.

(b) The words 'looked at' could replace the word 'scanned' in line 4. What additional idea does the word 'scanned' convey?

(c) What implication has the conjunction 'even though' in line 6?

(d) Suggest why the writer should describe Chris's hair as 'unruly' (l. 9–10) rather than 'untidy'.

(e) What impression of the solicitor does the writer give in referring to how he has parked his car?

(f) Why does the writer refer to Chris's attempt to 'edge' his car into the centre lane (l. 22) rather than to 'move' it there?

(g) What implication does Chris's statement 'You can say this much about Ingleton Crescent' (l. 24–25) suggest about his true opinion of the street?

(h) How can the expression 'loomed over it like a benevolent ogre' (l. 28) be suitably applied to Comstock Mill and Arkenshaw?

(i) Explain the use of italics for 'do' in line 35.

(*j*) By the end of the passage the reader has learned a good deal about the town of Arkenshaw. In what way does the writer provide this information gradually and naturally?

Third passage

Together we fought to grasp and lift the dolphin, and with some success, for we did drag and shove him a foot or so downshore. But the dolphin himself defeated us; frightened, possibly, of the man's presence, or hurt by our tugging and by the friction of sand and pebbles, he began to struggle,
5 spasmodically but violently; and at the end of the first strenuous minutes we had gained only a foot. I was exhausted, and Max Gale was breathing very hard.

'No good.' He stood back. 'He weighs a ton, and it's like trying to get hold of an outsize greased bomb. It'll have to be the rope. Won't it hurt him?'
10 'I don't know, but we'll have to try it. He'll die if he stays here.'

'True enough. All right, help me get it round the narrow bit above the tail.'

The dolphin lay like a log, his eye turning slowly back to watch us as we bent to tackle the tail rope. Without the torch it was impossible to tell, but I had begun to imagine that the eye wasn't so bright or watchful now. The tail
15 felt heavy and cold, like something already dead. He never flickered a muscle as we fought to lift and put a loop round it.

'He's dying,' I said, on a sort of gulp. 'That fight must have finished him.' I dashed the back of my hand over my eyes, and bent to the job. The rope was damp and horrible to handle, and the dolphin's tail was covered with coarse
20 sand.

'You do tear yourself up rather, don't you?'

I looked up at him as he worked over the loop. His tone was not ungentle, but I got the impression from it that half his mind was elsewhere: he cared nothing for the dolphin, but wanted merely to get this over, and get back
25 himself to whatever his own queer and shady night's work had been.

Well, fair enough. It was good of him to have come at all. But some old instinct of defensiveness made me say a little bitterly:

'It seems to me you can be awfully happy in this life if you stand aside and mind your own business, and let other people do as they like about damaging
30 themselves and one another. You go on kidding yourself you're impartial and tolerant and all that, then all of a sudden you realise you're dead, and you've never been alive at all. Being alive hurts.'

'So you have to break your heart over an animal who wouldn't even know you, and who doesn't even recognise you?'
35 'Someone has to bother,' I said feebly. 'Besides, he does recognise me, he knows me perfectly well.'

He let that one pass, straightening up from the rope. 'Well, there it is, that's the best we can do, and I'm hoping to heaven we can get it off again before he takes off at sixty knots or so . . . Well, here goes. Ready?'

18

(*a*) What do the words 'drag' and 'shove' in line 2 suggest about the two people's methods of attempting to move the dolphin?

(*b*) The dolphin is always referred to as 'he' and 'him'. What does this suggest about the story-teller's attitude towards the dolphin?

(*c*) Why should Max associate the dolphin with an 'outsize greased bomb' in line 9?

(*d*) What impression of the dolphin is given by the words 'lay like a log' (l.12)?

(*e*) What additional idea is conveyed by the words 'flickered a muscle' (l.15) as compared with 'moved a muscle'?

(*f*) What does the use of the word 'shady' in line 25 suggest about the nature of Max's night's work?

(*g*) Explain the connection between the story-teller's impression of Max in the paragraph starting in line 22 and her outburst two paragraphs later (l. 28–32).

(*h*) Why does the speaker use the emphatic form 'he does recognise me' in line 35?

(*i*) What contrast does the writer make between the two characters involved?

(*j*) What are three features of the direct speech in the passage which are characteristic of relaxed spoken language?

2 Reading comprehension

General advice about timing

You will probably decide to start with the vocabulary items in Section A. Read each sentence carefully, bearing in mind the various considerations detailed in Guidelines below. In certain cases the answer will be obvious; in others intelligent consideration will be needed but your final decision will be clear. Answers of this kind can be marked on the answer sheet at once, though in such a way that they can easily be changed later if necessary.

In some cases you may feel undecided, and in some have little or no idea of the answer. Do not linger over these answers: you have not enough time. You can return to these items after working on Section B; you may well find that the appropriate answer has come into your mind in the interval.

In Section B, read the first passage slowly and with intense concentration, taking up to 10 minutes on this. As you read each following item (again with concentration) try to refer it to what appears to be the corresponding section of the passage. Remember, however, that the obvious point of reference is not necessarily the right one, and also that more than one reference may be involved in the required information. Further advice is given about this in Guidelines. As in Section A, you may wish to leave certain items for later consideration though this may be less effective than in the vocabulary section as all the information is already in front of you: there is not the problem of recalling half-forgotten words and meanings to your mind.

Finally return to Section A and attempt the as yet undecided items. Do not leave any uncompleted: marks are not actually deducted for a wrong answer.

Timing this paper has to be flexible as you will probably follow the plan given here, i.e. a number of Section A items, most items on the Section B passages, a return to complete and check Section A, with final attention to Section B. So the rough 25-minute allocation for each of the three exercises will be difficult to observe though it could be borne in mind. If, as might happen, more than 2 reading comprehension passages are set, the 50 minutes available will have to be divided accordingly.

The most important factor is *to be aware of the time* in relation to what you have completed and what remains to be done. The time available is limited so do not waste any; on the other hand do not rush and lose the ability to concentrate.

A very loose timetable might be:

Section A: 15 minutes

20

Section B: 20–25 minutes for each passage (if there are only two)
This scheme would leave between 10 and 20 minutes for a reconsideration and checking of all answers.

Section A: Vocabulary Choice Sentences
Suggestions and advice

Nature of this test

40 multiple-choice questions designed to test knowledge of vocabulary and usage.

Guidelines

This section is designed to test lexis (vocabulary range), structure (as it influences word usage) and register (social, literary and other circumstances which make the use of one word preferable to that of another). Your choice will probably be determined by one or more of the following considerations.

1 Actual meaning of the given words and sentence.

   Example: He drove_____ as the road was icy.
   A rapidly **B** efficiently **C** heedlessly **D** courteously
   E cautiously
   Here the word *cautiously* is the word most likely to describe driving in icy conditions; *rapidly* might apply to some drivers but the use of *as* makes this very unlikely here. Though this is not common, *efficiently* could be applied to driving but it is far less likely and effective here than *cautiously*. *Heedlessly* and *courteously* are clearly out of place.

   Note: Words similar in form, and therefore confusing, may appear e.g. ingenious, genuine, generous, genial, genteel.

2 Relationships between words based on usage.

   Examples: a *barrier* to progress is a more usual phrase than a *deterrent* to progress.
   an operation is *performed* or *carried out*, not *made*.
   submit, not *offer*, an application for a post.
   a meeting that has to be continued later is *adjourned*, not *postponed* or *delayed*.
   confirm a suggested arrangement for a meeting, not *ratify, endorse* or *authenticate* it.

   Extensive reading is the only effective preparation for this kind of exercise.

3 Clues from the wording and structure of the sentence e.g. prepositions.

Example: He _____ on walking to work every day, however cold it was.
A   insisted   B   persisted   C   continued   D   believed
E   succeeded

In meaning, they could all apply, so here it is the structure of the sentence that must be considered closely. *Continued* is followed by the infinitive; *persisted, believed, succeeded* are followed by *in*; the answer must be *insisted*.

4   Phrasal verbs: the verb itself or the following particle.

Examples: Eastbound travellers have to _____ their watches forward as they enter a new time zone.
A   put   B   bring   C   set   D   turn   E   move
answer: put
Did the demonstration ever come _____ ?
A   off   B   across   C   round   D   out   E   up
answer: off

In cases of uncertainty, you can probably easily eliminate (take out) two or three words that are obviously unsuitable. This may leave you with two or at most three possibilities, and a very close examination of the formation and usage of each word may help you to arrive at the correct one.

Exercises

In this section you must choose the word or phrase which best completes each sentence. Write the number of each sentence and after it the letter A, B, C, D or E for the answer you choose. *Give one answer only* **to each question.**

Group 1

1   'You always give the best to Peter and never to me,' Derek _____ , 'and it isn't fair.'
A   explained   B   commented   C   complained   D   reported
E   demanded

2   Although his work was full of mistakes, he protested to his teacher about the poor _____ he had been given.
A   note   B   gradient   C   mark   D   level   E   standard

3   Your pronunciation would improve if you _____ with a tape recorder.
A   exercised   B   repeated   C   practised   D   trained   E   drilled

4   His total _____ as a full-time mechanic, part-time taxi-driver and week-end coach driver come(s) to more than £180 a week.
A   gains   B   salary   C   fees   D   profits   E   earnings

22

5 I am very much _____ your visit next week.
A anticipating   B looking forward to   C expecting
D foreseeing   E waiting for

6 Several burly policemen were needed to keep _____ the crowds when the new American rock group arrived.
A away   B down   C in   D back   E off

7 Next Thursday there will be an Old People's _____ to Brighton.
A journey   B travel   C excursion   D tour   E expedition

8 You cannot be given a rise until the standard of your work _____ .
A amends   B improves   C corrects   D betters   E mends

9 I made it quite clear that I had no _____ of selling the picture.
A meaning   B opinion   C purpose   D aim   E intention

10 We set light to some small _____ and then piled other wood on top.
A paper   B stalks   C twigs   D stems   E boughs

Group 2

1 After the voting slips had been counted, it was announced that Hammond had been _____ to parliament by a small majority.
A chosen   B voted   C selected   D preferred   E elected

2 The visiting professor gave a _____ about the early development of the novel in his country.
A lecture   B lesson   C conference   D speech   E sermon

3 Pennine Rovers _____ Cheviot Rangers in last Saturday's football match.
A won   B conquered   C gained   D beat   E overcame

4 He went down to his workshop in the _____ .
A loft   B ground floor   C attic   D basement
E conservatory

5 A policeman politely _____ me to move my car.
A ordered   B requested   C suggested   D begged   E urged

6 On this clear summer morning every leaf and blade of grass was sparkling with _____ .
A spray   B ripples   C sleet   D bubbles   E dew

7 I suppose I'll have to look for a job: _____ I'll either have to find a rich wife or starve.
A otherwise   B else   C conversely   D on the other hand
E on the contrary

8 I shall leave my suitcase in a luggage _____ at the station.
A box   B compartment   C wardrobe   D chest   E locker

9 Even before he got to the chemist's, he had lost the_____ for the medicine, and had to go back to the doctor to get another one.
A receipt   **B** remedy   **C** prescription   **D** recipe
E instructions

10 He tripped over a loose shoe-lace which he had not_____ tightly enough.
A pulled   **B** tied   **C** joined   **D** twisted   **E** fixed

Group 3

1 He has always been allowed to have his own_____ and now he is completely spoilt.
A wishes   **B** will   **C** desires   **D** way   **E** accord

2 We advise our customers to _____ advantage of our bargain prices during the coming week.
A make   **B** have   **C** get   **D** take   **E** enjoy

3 The warmth of the afternoon and the sweet scent of the flowers made me feel pleasantly_____ .
A intoxicated   **B** leisurely   **C** exhausted   **D** idle   **E** drowsy

4 Several experts have been called in to plan _____ for boating, tennis, refreshments and children's games in the projected town park.
A opportunities   **B** facilities   **C** advantages   **D** possibilities
E occasions

5 After a number of disagreements with the Committee, the Chairman has
_____.
A retired   **B** resigned   **C** dismissed   **D** deserted
E surrendered

6 You will find the correspondence with the Tax Authorities in the S to U
_____.
A file   **B** index   **C** register   **D** record   **E** briefcase

7 A few yellow and brown autumn leaves were _____ down the river.
A flowing   **B** swimming   **C** driving   **D** floating
E streaming

8 The captain realised that unless immediate action was taken to discipline the crew, there could be a_____ on the ship.
A mutiny   **B** rebellion   **C** strike   **D** revolution   **E** riot

9 I bought this eighteenth century writing-desk at a quite_____ price.
A reasonable   **B** cheap   **C** small   **D** expensive   **E** easy

10 These mats have been_____ from long narrow strips of old clothes.
A constructed   **B** woven   **C** knitted   **D** spun   **E** sown

1 The postman usually comes at about 8 o'clock with the first _____.
   A circulation   B distribution   C delivery   D postage
   E courier

2 Fruit is said to be _____ for me but I don't much like it.
   A healthy   B nourishing   C good   D appetising
   E satisfying

3 _____ of cattle could be grazed on these fertile plains.
   A swarms   B herds   C flocks   D packs   E shoals

4 There is nothing more _____ on an uncomfortably warm afternoon than
   a glass of ice-cold fruit juice.
   A relieving   B refreshing   C quenching   D relaxing
   E freshening

5 This woollen material should be dry-cleaned: it will _____ if you wash it
   in hot water.
   A shrink   B fade   C droop   D wither   E crease

6 Most of the machines are _____ as a result of an electrical breakdown.
   A out of work   B idle   C disused   D lazy   E powerless

7 Some of his suggestions have been adopted but others have been turned
   _____ as they are quite impracticable.
   A away   B back   C out   D down   E against

8 After such intensive training, the team's defeat in the Cup Final match was a
   keen _____ to them.
   A regret   B deception   C loss   D misfortune
   E disappointment

9 He was universally _____ for the accident, though it had not in fact been
   his fault.
   A accused   B blamed   C criticised   D condemned
   E slandered

10 _____ any remarriage this money would pass to your late husband's
   younger brother.
   A In the event of   B In accordance with   C As to   D With
   reference to   E On account of

Section B: Passages with Multiple-choice Questions
Suggestions and advice

Nature of this test
20 multiple-choice questions, based on two or more prose passages, designed to
test ability to read with comprehension.

Guidelines

The secret of reasonable success in this section depends on:
- (*a*) intense concentration in reading so that every smallest detail is noted
- (*b*) a refusal to be misled by some word or suggestion in the question, or any one of the responses

The correct response is quite likely to be expressed in different words though the meaning or information conveyed is the same. Beware of traps: there are various ones in this book.

The method of elimination can be used here also when you are very unsure. Check each response for its suitability: you can probably easily eliminate two of them. Then concentrate on the remaining two.

Bear in mind continually the time available.

Exercises

In this section you will find after each of the passages a number of questions or unfinished statements about the passage, each with four suggested answers or ways of finishing it. You must choose the one which you think fits best. Write the number of each question and after it the letter A, B, C or D for the answer you choose. *Give one answer only* to each question.

Read each passage right through before choosing your answers.

First passage

The snow in Norway falls in time for Christmas. It has to fall three times before it stays; then the white blanket that covers the mountain peaks spreads out over the whole land. A new kind of silence descends, and the Northern Lights move like shining coloured silk across the sky. Tall birch branches set
5 at intervals at the side of country roads guide the snow-ploughs that are ever on the move keeping the roads open—even a number of mountain routes that used to be closed until the snow melted. On other, less important mountain roads a barrier is lowered to show that there is no way through. Winter tyres, powerful car-heaters and getaway starting ensure that the motorist drives to
10 work as usual. Trains and buses run on time and get businessmen, office workers and schoolchildren to work at 8.30 a.m. A business day ends at 4 p.m.—the children start home at 2.30 after only the briefest of lunch-breaks. The dryness of the climate means that light, warm clothing keeps the cold out, and if you kick the snow you see it rise in a flurry of rice-like grains.
15 In December Oslo has a mean temperature of $-3°$ C, falling to $-4°$ in January and February and rising to zero in March.

From early December the Christmas trees—always hung with white lights—appear in the streets of towns and villages, giving off an almost ethereal glow in the snow. A particularly tall one is set up in the forecourt of
20 Oslo University, and as the holiday season draws near every Norwegian ship and fishing boat—sailing in home waters or far afield—will have a Christmas

tree on its mast. American-style designs have recently captured the Christmas card markets, but fortunately it is still possible to send and to receive the old Norwegian postcard-type. These have pictures of the *Julenisse* (Christmas
25 gnomes in scarlet caps with white beards), snowy farmsteads with horses, sleighs and brightly feathered winter birds that perch like coloured decorations on the snowy trees and feast on the sheaf of corn saved for them from the summer harvest and set up outside every farmhouse on Christmas Eve. This custom of giving not only the birds but every animal on the farm a
30 special titbit on Christmas Eve (the cows often get salted herring, which they like!) originates from the old belief that 'they were in the stable too'.

1　When does the snow first fall in Norway?

   A　Before Christmas
   B　At Christmas
   C　Around Christmas
   D　Before the Christmas period is over

2　The silence that follows the falling of the snow

   A　is deeper than before
   B　has a different quality to it
   C　is associated with the quietness of the falling snow
   D　is the silence normally experienced in snow-covered mountains

3　What impression is given of the Northern Lights?

   A　The colours keep changing to other colours
   B　They appear as stripes of colour
   C　They cast a hard and brilliant light
   D　There is a smooth floating effect of colour

4　How do the snow-ploughs find their way?

   A　They follow the track between the trees
   B　There are posts to indicate the edges of the road
   C　There are posts which point out the way
   D　A temporary fence is constructed for this purpose

5　The trains run

   A　punctually
   B　frequently
   C　exactly
   D　every hour

6　What information indicates the dryness of the winter climate?

   A　Temperatures are not unduly low for a northern country
   B　The type of clothing people have to wear
   C　The ease with which the snow powders
   D　The comparison between the snowflakes and grains of rice

7 What impression is given of the Christmas trees with their lights in Norway?

    A They can be seen almost everywhere
    B They cast a faint but beautiful light
    C They illuminate the falling snow
    D They glitter against the surrounding whiteness

8 What is the writer's attitude towards the typical Norwegian Christmas card?
    A She regards them as far more beautiful than American-style ones
    B She considers they give a true picture of Norway
    C She is glad they are still produced
    D She feels angry about their gradual disappearance

9 The fact that the Christmas feeding of the birds is a national tradition is suggested by

    A the places in which the corn is put
    B the saving of the sheaf of corn at harvest-time
    C the fact that it is corn that is given
    D the idea of feeding all the farm animals at Christmas time

Second passage

The third report on smoking and health from the Royal College of Physicians, which was published this month, contains important new sections on the smoking habits of children and the possible effects on their future health.

5   These include a twentyfold increase in the risk of lung cancer in heavy smokers and an increase of about three and a half times in the risk of dying from coronary heart disease; chronic bronchitis and emphysema are also much commoner. Teachers play an important part in determining the attitude of children to smoking, whether or not the children start to smoke, and in
10   providing knowledge about the consequences of smoking.

    Whenever I see children of school age openly smoking in public I wonder whether they really understand what they are doing. Probably most do not. I at least know that my clinical practice in lung disease will not be short of patients for the rest of my working life. About 34 per cent of boys aged 15
15   smoke, and two thirds this number of girls. Over the past 10 years there has been a small but welcome reduction in the number of boys who smoke at this age, but an increase in the number of girls.

    One large study has shown that of those children who smoke more than one cigarette, as many as 85 per cent become habitual smokers. This is partly
20   because nicotine is one of the most dependence-producing drugs known, on a par with heroin and other hard drugs in this respect. One in three smokers start before the age of nine, some even as young as five.

    The causes of premature death which one-third of smokers will suffer, and of the prolonged illnesses which affect so many of them, are described in the
25   report; it is enough to say that the younger a child starts to smoke the greater are his chances of dying early.

It has been shown that children who smoke have certain characteristics. Compared with non-smokers they are more rebellious, their work deteriorates as they move up school, they are more likely to leave school early, and are
30 more often delinquent and sexually precocious. Many of these features can be summarised as anticipation of adulthood.

There are a number of factors which determine the onset of smoking, and these are largely psychological and social. They include availability of cigarettes, curiosity, rebelliousness, appearing tough, anticipation of adult-
35 hood, social confidence, example of parents and teachers, and smoking by friends and older brothers and sisters.

It should be much easier to prevent children from starting to smoke than to persuade adults to give up the habit once established, but in fact this has proved very difficult. The example set by people in authority, especially
40 parents, health care workers, and teachers, is of prime importance. School rules should forbid smoking by children on the premises. This rule has even been introduced at Summerhill School where I spent my schooldays.

There is, however, a risk of children smoking just to rebel against the rules, and even in those schools which have tried to enforce no smoking by corporal
45 punishment there is as much smoking as in other schools. Nevertheless, banning smoking is probably on balance beneficial. Teachers too should not smoke on school premises, at least not in front of children.

1 According to the passage, the report on smoking
   A is mainly concerned with aspects of child smoking
   B compares the effects of smoking in children and in adults
   C introduces fresh material about smoking among children
   D deals for the first time with the effects of smoking among children

2 People who smoke heavily
   A run a twenty-to-one risk of contracting lung cancer
   B are almost certain to suffer from one or more of certain lung and heart complaints
   C are more prone than other people to certain lung or heart complaints
   D may possibly run more risk of contracting certain lung and heart diseases

3 Teachers can have a considerable influence on children's attitude towards smoking because
   A they are in a position to explain the risks the children will run
   B they can forbid the children to smoke
   C they can prevent them from starting to smoke
   D they are highly respected by the children

4 The writer of this article is by profession
   A a family doctor
   B a teacher

C medical specialist

D a journalist

5 What connection is suggested in the passage between smoking and heroin addiction?

A Smoking is almost as harmful as taking heroin

B Smoking should be considered as a form of hard drug addiction

C Smoking can become as much an addiction as taking heroin

D Smoking produces as powerful an effect as taking heroin

6 A regrettable feature of starting smoking in early childhood is that

A permanent dependence on smoking will be established

B it increases the risk of later drug addiction

C an adult is less likely to take up smoking than a child

D early smoking increases the risk of premature death

7 According to the passage a common characteristic of young smokers is that

A they have little respect for authority

B they are easily influenced in general by other people

C they have less than average intelligence

D they want to attract attention

8 The discouragement of smoking

A is more effective before the habit takes hold

B will be unsuccessful with confirmed smokers

C has had surprisingly little success with some children

D will be successful if children are forbidden to smoke

9 What measures should be taken by schools to dissuade children from smoking?

A Children should not be allowed to smoke in school

B Their teachers should be forbidden to smoke

C Care should be taken that the children never start smoking

D Children who smoke should be severely punished

10 According to the passage, one risk of banning smoking is that

A smoking may become a symbol of opposition to authority

B this would encourage more children to smoke in secret

C prohibition may cause an angry rebellion

D the ban will be ignored as being merely a school rule

11 What is the writer's assessment of the value of forbidding smoking?

A The effects of doing this will be worthwhile

B It may produce more good effects than harmful ones

C The advantages will probably be outweighed by the drawbacks

D It is a better idea than to encourage it

Third passage

I came across an old country guide the other day. It listed all the tradesmen in each village in my part of the country, and it was impressive to see the great variety of services which were available on one's own doorstep in the late Victorian countryside.

5 Nowadays a superficial traveller in rural England might conclude that the only village tradesmen still flourishing were either selling frozen food to the inhabitants or selling antiques to visitors. Nevertheless, this would really be a false impression. Admittedly there has been a contraction of village commerce, but its vigour is still remarkable.

10 Our local grocer's shop, for example, is actually expanding in spite of the competition from supermarkets in the nearest town. Women sensibly prefer to go there and exchange the local news while doing their shopping, instead of queueing up anonymously at a supermarket. And the proprietor knows well that personal service has a substantial cash value.

15 His prices may be a bit higher than those in the town, but he will deliver anything at any time. His assistants think nothing of bicycling down the village street in their lunch hour to take a piece of cheese to an old age pensioner who sent her order by word of mouth with a friend who happened to be passing. The more affluent customers telephone their shopping lists and the

20 goods are on their doorsteps within an hour. They have only to hint at a fancy for some commodity outside the usual stock and the grocer, a red-faced figure, instantly obtains it for them.

The village gains from this sort of enterprise, of course. But I also find it satisfactory because a village shop offers one of the few ways in which a

25 modest individualist can still get along in the world without attaching himself to the big battalions of industry or commerce.

Most of the village shopkeepers I know, at any rate, are decidedly individualist in their ways. For example, our shoemaker is a formidable figure: a thick-set, irritable man whom children treat with marked respect, knowing

30 that an ill-judged word can provoke an angry eruption at any time. He stares with smouldering contempt at the pairs of cheap, mass-produced shoes taken to him for repair: has it come to this, he seems to be saying, that he, a craftsman, should have to waste his skills upon such trash? But we all know he will in fact do excellent work upon them. And he makes beautiful shoes for

35 those who can afford such luxury.

1 The writer considered the old country guide interesting because he found in it

   A   the names of so many of the shops in the villages around

   B   the many people selling to, and doing jobs for, residents in local villages at the time it appeared

   C   the variety of shops and services available in Victorian days in Britain

   D   information about all the jobs there were in his own and surrounding villages at the time it appeared

2   The services available in villages nowadays are normally

    A   fewer but still very active
    B   less successful than earlier but managing to survive
    C   active in providing food for the villagers, and tourist goods
    D   surprisingly energetic considering the little demand for them

3   The local grocer's shop is expanding even though

    A   women spend a lot of their time there just gossiping
    B   town shops are larger and rather cheaper
    C   people like to shop where they are less well-known
    D   people get personal service in his shop

4   The writer implies that one disadvantage of town shops is that

    A   their prices are higher
    B   people cannot telephone them
    C   their staff may take less trouble to satisfy customers
    D   one has to queue up to pay in them

5   How do the village grocer's assistants feel about giving extra service?

    A   They tend to forget it
    B   They will not consider it
    C   They take it for granted
    D   It does not seem worth their while

6   Another aspect of personal service available in the village shop is that

    A   there is a very wide range of goods available
    B   rare goods are obtained whenever they are needed
    C   special attention is given to the needs of wealthier customers
    D   goods are always restocked before they run out

7   The writer approves of the village shop because

    A   he likes the idea that a humble person can be successful
    B   he welcomes competition with organised business
    C   this is a case of individual success in a world of increasing mass-production
    D   he welcomes an example of private enterprise surviving in an age of giant companies

8   In what way is the village shoemaker a 'formidable figure'?

    A   He seems to pay little attention to public opinion
    B   He will have nothing to do with inferior badly-produced shoes
    C   He has a very uncertain temper
    D   He has very high standards of workmanship

9   What is his reaction to mass-produced shoes?

    A   He considers they are not worth the effort of repairing properly
    B   He is angry with the customers for bringing in such rubbish
    C   He despises their quality
    D   He feels exasperated because people waste their money on inferior shoes

3 Use of English

General advice about timing

Although each section is quite different from the other two, an allocation of approximately one hour to each section is a reasonably satisfactory one. This is, however, only a rough guide. Candidates are likely to find one section easier and quicker to complete than the others. Moreover certain items in the first section in particular may require further consideration and a candidate may decide to leave these unanswered until after the other sections are completed. This is a sensible idea; in fact you should almost never spend a long time struggling with one item: leave it and come back to it later.

The same advice as that given in the case of Paper 2 applies here: be aware of timing. Pre-examination practice of timed answers to papers is therefore important: you need to have the feeling of approximately how long each answer is likely to take. Bear in mind throughout the paper how much more you have to do, how long this could take and how much time still remains.

Section A: Structural and Grammatical Exercises
Suggestions and advice

Nature of this test

According to the syllabus, this section is designed to test the candidate's active control of English usage and structure, and ability to manipulate the language at clause and sentence level. It will consist of open-completion items. The following four types of question normally appear in this section: gap filling, sentence transformation, sentence completion, transformation involving single given words.

Guidelines

1. *Gap filling*
Gaps (usually 20 in number) are left in a continuous prose passage and these normally have to be filled with a suitable single word. (Read the instructions carefully

33

however—the use of more than one word might at some time be required.)

Read through the whole passage considering possibilities as you do so. Normally you will not write anything until you have completed the first reading.

The second reading is more intensive and some, possibly most, of the words can be recorded now. Do not pause too long over any one word: you can return to it in a third reading or when you have completed the whole paper.

While some of the words to be supplied may be classed as vocabulary items in certain contexts, the main emphasis will be on grammatical and structural forms. Words commonly confused such as *make/do, possibility/opportunity* may be involved; singular or plural forms (e.g. *the police* followed by a plural verb form); commonly confused constructions such as *so that/so as, or/nor*; suitable prepositions; a choice of a definite article or possessive adjective or omission of the article: any of these and other doubtful examples of usage may be featured.

2. *Sentence transformation*

A given sentence is followed by the opening of an apparently different sentence. As the same meaning is to be expressed in this second sentence, the construction of the first one must be transformed to follow satisfactorily the new beginning.

(*a*) Read the given sentence carefully so as to understand the meaning to be expressed—the EXACT meaning and ALL the meaning.

Example: I had some difficulty in understanding what he said.
It was . . . .

Reference to the elements *I* and *some*, suitably transposed, must form part of the new sentence:
It was rather difficult for me to understand what he said.

(*b*) You now have to search for a structural form with the new beginning which will express the full and exact meaning.

Examples: (i) 'Will you help me?' he asked.
He asked . . . .
(reported question form)
He asked me $\left\{ \begin{matrix} \text{if} \\ \text{whether} \end{matrix} \right\}$ I would help him.

(ii) He claimed I had stolen the money.
He accused . . . .
(*accused*—followed by personal object + gerund construction)
He accused me of having stolen the money.

(iii) Man has always wished he could fly.
Man has always wanted . . . .
(*wanted*—followed by infinitive: here *to be able*)
Man has always wanted to be able to fly.

34

The best preparation for this answer is the widest possible practice beforehand with grammatical and structural exercises, not necessarily all of the kind used in this section.

3. *Sentence completion*

A gap within or at the end of a sentence has to be filled with a suitable word or phrase.

The meaning of the words to be added is made clear from the words given. The addition must conform grammatically and structurally with its context. Some of the features most commonly tested in this exercise are verb tenses (including those used in conditions); modal verbs and their significance; gerund, infinitive and clause constructions; forms of ellipsis including short answers; question tags and end verb forms ('He'll come but I *won't*').

In deciding the form of the additional word or word group, study the words given before and after and try to discover what is being tested. This could be the use of the present perfect continuous tense with *since*, the present tense form after *as soon as*, or the gerund after *looking forward to*, for example.

The exercise is largely concerned with what are known to be common structural errors, so beware of being caught.

4. *Transformation involving single given words*

This type of exercise is a variant of No. 2. There is the same necessity for careful study of meaning and expressing the same meaning with a different structure, in this case one incorporating the given word.

Example: An accident seemed inevitable   AVOID
It seemed impossible to avoid an accident.

Notice that the exact word given must be used, not a related verbal or negative form or part of speech.

Exercises

1. Fill each of the numbered blanks in the following passages with *one* suitable word.

1 (*a*) The _____ (1) day, some two or three days ago actually, I visited my sister in hospital. She is _____ (2) than I am: in fact she was almost grown-up when I _____ (3) born. She had _____ (4) a minor operation but was reported to have largely got _____ (5) the after-effects of this. My wife suggested _____ (6) taking her some flowers and fruit but she said that I _____ (7) not take her any books as she herself had given her a lot _____ (8). This was my first visit so it _____ (9) me several minutes to locate the ward she was in. I always find hospital visiting _____ (10) of an ordeal, and as I walked between the _____ (11) of

35

beds, I felt _____ (12) depressed, especially at the sight of the lonely patients, those _____ (13) friends had not turned _____ (14) to chat with them. My sister was half-sitting, half-_____ (15), propped up on pillows, with a paperback detective story in _____ (16) hand. She put aside the book, a little reluctantly it seemed, thanked me in a rather half-hearted way for the gifts and _____ (17) me silently while I took a _____ (18) on the hard wooden chair by her bedside. I commented _____ (19) how well she looked but she ignored my remark. 'Tell me,' she burst out unexpectedly, 'if you were a doctor and wanted to _____ (20) a murder, one of your patients, of course, how would you do it?'

1 (b) For the small boy, the model car, repeatedly wound _____ (1), and later perhaps electrically propelled, is a favourite _____ (2). So when, _____ (3) a young man, he actually has the _____ (4) of sitting in _____ (5) own vehicle and _____ (6) it himself, he knows he has at last found what he has really been waiting to play with. _____ (7) from using it merely for the _____ (8) of driving, spending large sums _____ (9) petrol in order to get nowhere in _____ (10), his main delight is _____ (11) taking the engine _____ (12) pieces in order to put it _____ (13) again. His unfortunate girl friend may be _____ (14) to death by interminable accounts of how he has _____ (15) to discover the _____ (16) of the slight oil leak while his mother hears with misgiving about alarming distances _____ (17) in record _____ (18). The passage of years alas converts this symbol of daring, unfettered youth _____ (19) the status symbol of middle age, regularly serviced at the garage, and now merely a docile means of _____ (20) for the family on Sunday outings to in-laws, or for himself on the daily journey to the office.

2 **Finish each of the following sentences in such a way that it means exactly the same as the sentence printed before it.**
Example: There were trees on all sides of the house.
             The house was ....
Answer: The house was surrounded by trees.

2 (a) 1 I didn't deal with the problem that evening as it was too late.
          It was too ....

       2 He lived so far from his job that he decided to move nearer.
          He lived such ....

       3 He will inherit the estate on his twenty-first birthday.
          He will inherit the estate as ....

       4 It was too dark for us to see our way properly.
          It was so ....

5 My father thought it would be a good idea for us all to have a holiday together.
My father wanted . . . .

6 You could have left some of the chocolate for me.
You need . . . .

7 Far from being annoyed by my late arrival, he was considerably relieved to see me.
I had expected him . . . .

8 Why didn't you let me know you were coming?
You might . . . .

9 He was one of my father's lifelong friends.
He was a . . . .

10 He told everybody except his wife about his promotion.
His wife . . . .

2 (b) 1 I find it very difficult to remember people's names.
Remembering . . . .

2 He spent two hours doing the washing-up.
It took . . . .

3 I warned him against climbing in weather like this.
I told him it . . . .

4 We had not expected him to arrive so early.
His arrival was . . . .

5 There seemed to be no reason for his intense nervousness.
We could not understand why . . . .

6 They were astonished at how big the garden was.
They were astonished at the . . . .

7 She offered me a cup of tea.
She said to me, ' . . . .?'

8 However long it takes you, you must read the book right through.
Even though . . . .

9 I was next disturbed by a hammering from the flat above.
It was . . . .

10 'Will you have lunch with us tomorrow?' my friends asked me yesterday.
Yesterday my friends invited . . . .

2 (c) 1 He slipped the money into his pocket unseen.
Nobody noticed him . . . .

2 My dog is always disobedient.
My dog never does . . . .

3 The hairdresser charged me less than usual for the shampoo and set.
   The hairdresser did not . . . .

4 What surprises me is that nobody heard the shot.
   The fact . . . .

5 It may be possible for us to visit the museum tomorrow.
   We may have . . . .

6 A donkey is the same as an ass.
   There is no . . . .

7 They were trying to discover the origin of the fire.
   They were trying to discover how . . . .

8 I should be very grateful if would would move your car forward a little.
   Would you be so . . . .

9 As he becomes more famous, he behaves more childishly.
   The more famous . . . .

10 Children may learn to pronounce a foreign language by imitating their
   teacher's speech.
   Children may learn to pronounce a foreign language by speaking in

   . . . .

3 Fill each of the numbered blanks with *one* suitable word or phrase.

Example: I've telephoned the house several times but nobody seems

. . . .

Answer: to be at home, to be there

3 (*a*) 1 I noticed there was a radio in my hotel room, so, wanting to hear the
           news, I . . . .

        2 You may be requested to state your place of birth or, more simply, just
           be asked, 'Where . . . .?'

        3 A French film was being shown in our town last week so I asked our
           French guest if he would be interested . . . . .cinema.

        4 According to the reviews, the new play is so boring that it isn't worth
           . . . .

        5 Moira: 'Would you enjoy playing tennis or would you prefer to go
           swimming?'
           Magda: 'The water might be quite cold today so I'd rather
           . . . .'

        6 Have you left anything in the oven? I can smell . . . .

        7 Jane: 'He spoke to me for the first time this morning.'
           Jill: 'Really! What . . . . .to you?'

        8 Rain, snow, hail, sleet and bitter cold at midsummer. What
           . . . .!

3 (*b*) 1 I didn't quite understand what you just said. Would you be so kind
.... again?'

2 I shall let you know my opinion in my letter the next time I
.... you.

3 Giles: 'Will you be spending next Sunday in the country?'
George: 'Well, we should very much ...., but we must do
some work in the garden.'

4 Mother: 'Your hair is getting rather long.'
Dick: 'Yes, I know. If I'd had time yesterday, I'd have gone to the
barber's and ....'

5 I last saw your daughter eight years ago so I'm very much looking
forward ....

6 I can't see to untie this knot without my glasses. Could you
.... me?

7 Miss Jenkins, would you please show me the letter you're typing now as
soon .... it.

8 Janet may not want to go to the circus but I ....

3 (*c*) 1 We had a meal in the Strandview Restaurant yesterday. Jessica didn't
enjoy it and nor ....

2 There are some heavy black clouds coming up from the west. I think I'll
take a mackintosh as it looks as ....

3 Christmas Day is the twenty- ....

4 Douglas: 'Where shall we go for our summer holiday?'
Dorothy: 'Well, the Cornish coast is beautiful. How about
..............?'

5 On days when he thinks he is going to have a school test, he sometimes
pretends to be ill in order to avoid the necessity ....

6 It's extremely cold out and your cough sounds worse this morning. I
really wouldn't go out if I .... you.

7 My dog takes no notice when I order him not to do something. I wish I
could make ....

8 You need not have taken a bus for that short distance. You could
....

9 I told him that the second-hand car for sale was worthless, but he
thought it was a bargain and insisted ....

**4 For each of the sentences below, write a new sentence as *similar as possible in
meaning to the original sentence*, but using the word given in capital letters.**

Example: He did not answer immediately.
HESITATED

Answer: He hesitated before answering.

4 (*a*)   1   He repeatedly asked unnecessary questions.
          KEPT

           2   Jane's mother requested that her daughter should be given extra homework.
          WANTED

           3   He never stops grumbling about how hard he has to work.
          ALWAYS

           4   The Bromleys got someone to instal central heating in their flat.
          HAD

           5   Yesterday she had a lot of revision to do for her examination.
          BUSY

           6   It's too cold to go out for a picnic today.
          WARM

           7   An election is expected in the autumn.
          PROBABLY

           8   It wasn't necessary for you to spend all that money on a long-distance call.
          NEED

           9   A farmer let us pitch our tent in one of his fields.
          PERMISSION

         10   I'm glad I'll see you tomorrow.
          FORWARD

4 (*b*)   1   My headmaster advised me to apply for a university grant.
          SUGGESTED

           2   They got married in 1970.
          SINCE

           3   He carried a torch so as not to lose his way in the dark.
          THAT

           4   Were you able to get the job you applied for?
          SUCCEED

           5   They've been talking continuously for two hours.
          STOPPED

           6   One can get to Glasgow in eight hours.
          JOURNEY

           7   It was difficult for me to make out the faded writing.
          DIFFICULTY

           8   This is the coldest winter we've ever experienced.
          SUCH

9 He didn't realise what a long way he would have to walk.
HOW

10 You don't need to buy more food.
THERE

Section B: Comprehension
Suggestions and advice

Nature of this test

According to the examination syllabus, this test consists of questions on a passage designed to test ability to understand, interpret and summarise.

Comparison with the Comprehension exercise on Paper 1
The emphasis in questions on the Paper 3 passage is on:

    (*a*) the understanding, extraction and reproduction of information presented in the passage.

    (*b*) the meaning and application of this information

    (*c*) meanings of expressions, and the application of this meaning to the passage

    (*d*) the ability to summarise.

Broadly speaking, therefore, this Comprehension exercise is concerned mainly with the information being presented while the exercise on Paper 1 is concerned with *how* it is presented.

Types of questions asked

    (*a*) General comprehension questions which require the extraction and possibly the explanation and reframing of information. These may be designed to elicit a single piece of information

    e.g. What was the immediate result of _____ ?

    or cover a wider field involving different parts of the passage

    e.g. What evidence is there for _____ ?

    (*b*) Certain expressions from the passage may be given. Their application to ideas in the passage has to be explained

    e.g. Why are the forests referred to as 'green gold'?

    or: What features of the proposed scheme justify the description 'gilt without the gingerbread'?

    The explanation must *always* be found in the passage.

(c) Meanings of words and word groups in their context. This may require
either (i) an explanation of the word or word group
or (ii) an alternative means of expression

(d) Meanings and applications of an expression other than the ones applicable in the passage.

(e) Selection of an expression from the passage which conveys certain information or meaning.

(f) Changes of meaning resulting from certain changes in a word group e.g. by the omission of words.

(g) The identifying of certain terms—pronouns or other parts of speech such as *the matter under discussion* or *this solution*. These must be explained by supplying the information in the passage they refer to. The same applies to pronouns such as *this* and *it*, which must be referred to the ideas they are taking the place of.

In many cases the exact words needed are not in the passage: the candidate must supply his own words to express the relevant ideas.

(h) Explanations of the use of such features as inverted commas and italics, not as an indication of the writer's technique but as a matter of usage.

(i) Summarising of a theme, reasons, evidence etc. developed in the passage.

Guidelines

1 Timing and answer length: keep within a time-limit of one hour and restrict your answer to the number of lines allowed on the answer paper.

2 Read through the passage carefully, and then fairly rapidly through the questions to get a general idea of what you have to do.

3 You can answer the questions in any order so you will probably prefer to deal first with those you can manage easily.

4 Distinguish between *explaining* what a word group means and *replacing* it by another one.

5 In the case of meaning changes within an expression, either:

   (a) only the modifying influence of the particular words referred to may have to be explained,

   e.g. Prices on the whole have remained stationary.
   on the whole suggests that a few prices have not remained stationary.

   (b) the point of contrast may have to be made clear by a brief indication of both meanings relevant to the contrast.

6 Distinguish between a direct quotation you must make from the passage and supplying your own words to express information given in the passage.

7 When identifying certain terms and pronouns (see (g) above), you may not find the answer as a specific single term, but may have to supply your own term to express this information,

   e.g. *this* refers to a plan to improve the reading standards of illiterate people

8 When information has to be selected from the passage and used to answer a question make sure that

   (*a*)   you understand the exact purpose of the question
   (*b*)   you include *all* the information needed
   (*c*)   you express it in such a way that it relates exactly to the question

In certain types of answers, as for example in providing evidence for a statement, you may have to give careful thought to deciding exactly what constitutes *evidence*.

Summarising

The summary is rarely if ever a précis of the whole passage. It is in fact an account involving the selection of relevant details in answer to certain questions.

Here are some possible instructions that may be given:

_____   describe the process which _____
_____   explain the extent to which _____
_____   explain the possible effects of the scheme _____
_____   state the evidence given in the passage for supposing _____

The material for answering the question will all be found in the passage: you must not introduce other material, however relevant and useful.

The number of words to be used is stated as a helpful guide to the scope of the answer, to discourage too short, or too elaborate, an answer. 'About 100 words' can be interpreted roughly as between 90 and 110, but not 75 or 132. Marks can be lost by failure to observe the instructions.

1 Read the question extremely carefully; you may like to note down on rough paper exactly what you will be looking for.
2 You will already be familiar with the passage but read it again, noting down those points of information which answer the question, those points which *'explain'*, *'illustrate'*, *'describe'*, the *'process'*, *'reasons'*, *'effects'*, *'evidence'* referred to. While it may appear that all the relevant matter appears in one section of the passage, do not take this for granted. Some useful idea may be hidden elsewhere—so glance right through.
3 Check that you have discovered all the required details.
4 A summary is written in sentences and paragraph form—not as notes. On rough paper you now embody your points in grammatically-correct sentence form.
5 While individual words from the passage are likely to appear in your answer, the whole effect should be of a reproduction of information in your own words. A good summary is *not* just the bringing together of word groups already existing in the passage.
6 As you write, be aware of the number of words at your disposal. Practice will help you to develop a feeling for whether you are overrunning your word

resources at each stage of the summary. It is a useful idea to check your word total at the end of each sentence. Even so the final total may be (i) too large or (ii) too small. You now work on the answer (i) finding ways of more concise expression or omitting less essential details (ii) introducing less essential but still relevant details (but not merely extra non-essential words).

7 Having achieved a satisfactory word total, examine your rough answer again with a view to
  (*a*) correcting grammatical, spelling and other mistakes
  (*b*) making improvements in choice of words, word order and sentence construction, expression in general.

8 When you are reasonably satisfied with your answer, copy it into the space provided. Check finally for any copying and other previously unnoticed faults.

Pre-examination practice: Summarising is, for many students, a new kind of exercise, and therefore needs a very great deal of practice before the examination. It can become a state of mind whereby you accustom yourself to making a mental summary of many things that you hear or read. A good deal of practice of the examination-type summaries is included in this book, and as you gain experience you can find passages of similar difficulty elsewhere and devise your own summary question. A lot of practice can be done on your own: you can acquire greater speed and facility. But you will quite certainly need the advice of a teacher who will be able to assess your work, show you any misinterpretations of the exercise you have done, and suggest ways of improving.

Passages for Comprehension

Read the following passages and then answer the questions which follow them.

Model questions and answers

If inclusive holiday bookings for the popular overseas destinations are anything to go by, then this is the year when many people—and especially families—will choose to holiday at home. A lot of them will head for a hotel, boarding house or apartment in one of the traditional resorts; but others, un-
5 der the firm but not always accurate impression that it is cheaper, will simply load up the family car and go where the fancy takes them.

The reason why that may not turn out to be a cheap holiday after all is that a great many other people will almost certainly have had the same idea. Cheap overnight accommodation will be at a premium, especially in the pop-
10 ular holiday areas and along the main holiday routes. In Scotland, for example, it is almost impossible to find a reasonably-priced overnight room in the summer months after about 4 p.m. or 5 p.m.—and latecomers have to choose between an expensive hotel or a chilly and distinctly uncomfortable night in the car.

15   Clever tourists will avoid such expense and discomfort by planning their itinerary so that they can stay with friends and relatives, but for those who value their friends, or cannot stand their family, there is another answer: take your overnight home with you.

    That can mean something as simple as a tent in the boot of a car, or as
20 complicated as a huge luxury trailer which would be better suited (and far less of a nuisance to the other road users) on a static site.

    For most people, however, it will mean a small caravan capable of being towed in comfort and safety by the average family car. And the latest improvements in caravans, especially as far as weight and internal lay-out are
25 concerned, mean that you can hire or buy a comfortable caravan suitable for four or five people without having to couple it to a big car.

    Even better, perhaps, is a motor caravan—although I would always prefer to combine the use of one of these with a tent because of the space problem, especially as far as headroom is concerned. Although they are expensive to
30 buy or convert, motor caravans can be hired relatively cheaply and are increasingly popular.

    Another form of caravan holiday is, of course, the static caravan on a permanent site. This is probably the cheapest form of self-catering holiday that there is, but some caravan-fleet owners have spoilt the market by providing
35 drab or overcrowded sites which have given a static caravan holiday a somewhat sordid image. Static caravans can also be very claustrophobic in bad weather—and you cannot move in search of the sun.

1   Explain the contrast between the two kinds of holiday in one's own country referred to in the first paragraph.

One alternative is to spend the whole time in a hotel or other accommodation at a holiday resort. The other is a mobile holiday, travelling without any fixed plan in the family car and thus spending each night in a different place.

2   'are anything to go by' in lines 1–2 can be otherwise expressed as provide reliable information

3   The words 'head for' in line 3 suggest that the people who do this set out with the deliberate intention of going there.

4   The 'traditional resorts' (line 4) are places which have attracted holidaymakers for many years.

5   People who 'go where the fancy takes them' (line 6) spend their holidays travelling wherever they feel like going, without making any fixed plan.

6   The words 'after all' in line 7 imply that the fact that the holiday is not cheap is unexpected.

7 'at a premium' (line 9) suggests that the cheap overnight accommodation is of special value because of the competition to get it.

8 What must the family touring by car in Scotland in the summer season do if they hope to find an inexpensive room for the night? They must start looking for it in the afternoon.

9 What is implied by the suggestion that people who value their friends (line 17) should need 'another answer'? Providing accommodation for a touring family may be regarded as a nuisance and result in the end of the friendship.

10 Why should people who 'cannot stand their family' (line 17) avoid staying with relatives? They dislike their relatives too much to wish to stay with them.

11 'take your overnight home with you' (lines 17–18) is an alternative answer to the problem of how to be sure of getting cheap overnight accommodation.

12 The luxury trailer referred to in line 20 would be a nuisance on the road because it would take up too much space and block the traffic behind it.

13 A static site (line 21) is a place where caravans can remain permanently.

14 Explain what each of the following words refers to:
'it' (line 5)   touring in the family car
'that' (line 7)   touring in the family car
'such expense' (line 15)   the cost of staying in an expensive hotel.
'that' (line 19)   your overnight home

15 The internal lay-out of the caravan referred to in line 24 is the way in which the furniture and equipment are arranged.

16 The space problem mentioned in line 28 refers to the fact that there is not much room in a motor caravan and it may not be high enough for tall people's comfort.

17 On a self-catering holiday (line 33) people provide for all their own needs apart from accommodation.

18 Static caravans can be claustrophobic in bad weather (lines 36–37) because the occupants may not want to go out but feel imprisoned in the small space available.

19 Explain why, according to the passage, more people are taking touring holidays nowadays and, as a result, why it may be advisable to have a tent or caravan available when touring. Use about 100 words.

It is a common belief that a touring holiday in the family car is less expensive than staying in a hotel or other accommodation in a holiday resort. Accordingly this kind of touring is very popular nowadays. As a result there is a very considerable demand for overnight accommodation during the summer, particularly in attractive areas and along touring routes, so that the choice lies between seeking overnight lodging in the afternoon, paying a high price for it or sleeping uncomfortably in the car. Staying with friends or relatives may prove unsatisfactory. The problem is solved however if a tent or caravan can be used.   (105 words)

Practice passages

First passage

Road research experts, baffled by 'motorway madness', are to make an attempt to discover why drivers continue to take fatal risks in mist and fog. Studies of motorway accidents have revealed startling evidence that 98 per cent of drivers ignore all warnings of imminent danger, particularly fog.

5   After two years of computerised research into driving and crashes, Dr. Peter Lewis, a lecturer at Birmingham University department of transportation, says: 'The positive fright of a crash or a very near miss appears to be the only thing which will make a driver more careful.'

His findings coincide with those of experts in the Department of the En-
10 vironment, who have persuaded Dr. John Gilbert, Minister of Transport, to authorise the latest of a series of projects to stop the slaughter resulting from multiple crashes on motorways.

Next month, a £5,000 American automatic speed-recording machine that photographs vehicles exceeding a set speed will be installed on a stretch of the
15 M4 near Reading—known to be particularly fog-prone. The machine, called Orbis, takes a photograph of the vehicle and its number plate, and records its speed, the time and the date. It can record up to 900 vehicles an hour in a 24-hour period.

Similar machines are used in Germany and the US as speed traps, but Dr.
20 Gilbert is determined the Orbis will be used only for experiment by the Transport and Road Research Laboratory.

Dr. Gilbert said last week: 'We shall use the machine to identify drivers who drive fast in fog. The department will then write to them and invite them to complete a questionnaire and perhaps take part in some physical tests.' He
25 added, 'One of the most interesting aspects of the research so far is that some motorists can see appreciably better than others in fog.'

It is already known that the driver who can see best is not necessarily the fastest, but a well-sighted driver frequently gathers behind him a convoy of vehicles whose drivers are frantically trying to keep his tail lights in view,

30   despite the advice contained in the motorway fog code which states: 'Don't
       hang on to someone else's tail lights. It gives a false sense of security.'

1   What is being referred to here by the expression 'motorway madness' (line
     1)? . . . .

2   'Fatal' risks (line 2) are ones which result in . . . .

3   The evidence revealed is described as 'startling' (line 3) because the figures
     show that . . . .

4   The expression 'imminent danger' (line 4) suggests some kind of disaster
     that . . . .

5   A multiple crash (line 12) is one . . . .

6   If a stretch of road is known to be 'fog-prone' (line 15) accidents there may
     be more frequent because . . . .

7   Explain in your own words the difference in purpose between Orbis and
     similar speed-recording machines used in Germany and the United States.
     . . . .

8   In the sentence beginning in line 23, what two words suggest that the drivers'
     co-operation will be voluntary? . . . .

9   Information given in the passage suggests that one of the physical tests given
     will involve . . . .

10   Two words that could be inserted between 'is' and 'that' in line 25 are
     . . . .

11   When a group of vehicles is referred to as a 'convoy' (line 28), there is a
     suggestion that they are close together because . . . .

12   Why is the word 'frantically' (line 29) used to describe the following drivers'
     attempt to keep the tail lights in view? . . . .

13   In general, what kind of advice would you expect to find in the motorway fog
     code? (line 30) . . . .

14   When a driver 'hangs on to' (line 31) someone else's tail lights, what he is
     doing is to . . . .

15   In a paragraph of not more than 100 words explain why the experts have
     decided to experiment with the Orbis machine, how it will be able to identify
     speeding drivers, and what action will then be taken . . . .

Second passage

     For an hour Rollo Martins waited, walking up and down to keep warm, inside the
     enclosure of the Great Wheel; the smashed Prater[1] with its bones sticking crudely
     through the snow was nearly empty. One stall sold thin flat cakes like cartwheels,
     and the children queued with their coupons. A few courting couples would be
5   packed together in a single car of the Wheel and revolve slowly above the city,
     surrounded by empty cars. As the car reached the highest point of the Wheel, the
     revolutions would stop for a couple of minutes and far overhead the tiny faces
     would press against the glass. Martins wondered who would come for him. Was
     there enough friendship left in Harry for him to come alone, or would a squad of
10   police arrive? It was obvious from the raid on Anna Schmidt's flat that he had a

[1] Prater—a large fairground in Vienna.

certain pull. And then as his watch hand passed the hour, he wondered: Was it all an invention of my mind? Are they digging up Harry's body now in the Central Cemetery?

15 Somewhere behind the cake stall a man was whistling, and Rollo knew the tune. He turned and waited. Was it fear or excitement that made his heart beat—or just the memories that tune ushered in, for life had always quickened when Harry came, came just as he came now, as though nothing much had happened, nobody had been lowered into a grave or found with cut throat in a basement, came with his amused, deprecating, take-it-or-leave-it

20 manner—and of course one always took it.

'Harry.'

'. . . Hallo, Rollo,'

'We've got to talk, Harry.'

'Of course.'

25 'Alone'

'We couldn't be more alone than here.'

He had always known the ropes, and even in the smashed pleasure park he knew them, tipping the woman in charge of the Wheel, so that they might have a car to themselves. He said, 'Lovers used to do this in the old days, but

30 they haven't the money to spare, poor devils, now,' and he looked out of the window of the swaying, rising car at the figures diminishing below with what looked like genuine commiseration.

Very slowly on one side of them the city sank; very slowly on the other the great cross-girders of the Wheel rose into sight. As the horizon slid away the

35 Danube became visible, and the piers of the Kaiser Friedrich Brücke lifted above the houses. 'Well,' Harry said, 'it's good to see you, Rollo.'

'I was at your funeral, Harry.'

'That was pretty smart of me, wasn't it?'

'Not so smart for your girl. She was there too—in tears.'

40 'She's a good little thing,' Harry said. 'I'm very fond of her.'

'I didn't believe the police when they told me about you.'

Harry said, 'I wouldn't have asked you to come if I'd known what was going to happen, but I didn't think the police were on to me.'

'Were you going to cut me in on the spoils?'

45 'I've never kept you out of anything, old man, yet.' He stood with his back to the door as the car swung upwards, and smiled back at Rollo Martins, who could remember him in just such an attitude in a secluded corner of the school quad, saying, 'I've learned a way to get out at night. It's absolutely safe. You are the only one I'm letting in on it.' For the first time Rollo Martins looked back

50 through the years without admiration, as he thought: he's never grown up. . . . Evil was like Peter Pan—it carried with it the horrifying and horrible gift of eternal youth.

Martins said, 'Have you ever visited the children's hospital? Have you seen any of your victims?'

55 Harry took a look at the toy landscape below and came away from the

49

door. 'I never feel quite safe in these things,' he said. He felt the back of the door with his hand, as though he were afraid that it might fly open and launch him into that iron-ribbed space. 'Victims?' he asked. 'Don't be melodramatic, Rollo. Look down there,' he went on, pointing through the window at the
60 people moving like black flies at the base of the Wheel. 'Would you really feel any pity if one of those dots stopped moving—for ever? If I said you can have twenty thousand pounds for every dot that stops, would you really, old man, tell me to keep my money—without hesitation? Or would you calculate how many dots you could afford to spare? Free of income tax, old man. Free
65 of income tax.' He gave his boyish conspiratorial smile. 'It's the only way to save nowadays.'

1 The 'bones sticking crudely through the snow' (lines 2–3) are the
   . . . .

2 The stall mentioned in line 3 is referred to again later when
   . . . .

3 What would be the main reason for visitors' wanting to go on the Great
   Wheel? . . . .

4 The faces pressing against the glass were tiny (lines 7–8) because . . . .

5 The word 'he' in line 10 refers to . . . ., while 'his' in line 11 refers
   to . . . .

6 'He had a certain pull' (lines 10–11) could be otherwise expressed as
   . . . .

7 What follows the words 'He had always known the ropes' (line 27) suggests that
   this expression means . . . .

8 What would cause the horizon apparently to 'slide away' (line 34)?
   . . . .

9 What two other phrases between line 33 and line 36 describe the same effect
   as 'the horizon slid away' (line 34)? . . . .

10 What do you understand by 'that' in line 38? . . . .

11 Explain in your own words a possible effect of evil on a person's nature as
   this is suggested in lines 49–52 . . . .

12 Why are people described as moving 'like black flies' at the base of the wheel
   (line 60)? . . . .

13 In what way did Harry use the smallness of the people to justify his completely callous attitude towards them? . . . .

14 Sum up in about 100 words the various impressions you have gained from
   the passage of the kind of person Harry is . . . .

Third passage

I was born in the East End of London and grew up there during the Depression of the early thirties. My father died when I was four years old and our mother
had to bring up three children. She did not have a pension, and there were no

social benefits, so she worked. She ran a coffee shop, opposite the number ten

5 gate of the London docks—not one of those smart places which became popular after the war, but a 'caff'—or what was then known as a good pull-up for
car-men.

We were lucky; we had enough to eat. But by any standard, Shadwell in
those days was a grim place to grow up in. It was a parish of tenements,
10 terraced cottages and dock walls. There could not have been a poorer place in
Britain. I afterwards read George Orwell's book, *The Road to Wigan Pier*,
which recorded his early experiences of the urban poor, and wondered why he
made such a fuss. Unemployment was widespread, and the dole for a married
man was about a pound a week. The only work available, apart from going to
15 sea, was in the docks as a casual labourer. The dockers were hired for only a
half-day's work at at time. They used to line up outside our shop in the early
morning, ragged and shivering in winter, and the foreman came along and
hired the strong ones. The remainder, a large majority, drifted away to the
meagre warmth of the public library. Most of the kids who went to my school
20 were underfed, and looked it. The basic diet was bread and meat-fat—bought
at the butcher's for two pence a bowl. A pennyworth of chips was a Friday
night treat.

The tenements were old, bug-ridden and over-crowded. Our street was
known as Incubator Street because it was always swarming with children.
25 There was no National Health, and few social services. It sounds dreadful,
but it was not: I did not know that I was poor or underprivileged, or whatever
the euphemism then was. Looking back without sentimentality, it was an
experience which had a beneficial influence on my life and career. If I may put
aside false modesty, I became a journalist, and a good journalist, because of
30 that early experience.

As a foreign correspondent of *The Times*, I covered some of the great
stories of our times. I met the great and not so great, those who made news
and the true men of destiny. I cannot say that I was overawed by them. I
recognised the truly great men, and gave them credit for their greatness, but
35 in my simple, direct, cockney fashion I treated them as equals. I lived among
many races, and in different cultures. I dined with presidents, kings and prime
ministers and went hungry and was shot at on more than one battlefield. I
wrote books and won awards. More important, I enjoyed life immensely; and
mainly because of my first and major experience of growing up poor in
40 London.

1 How would a pension and social benefits have helped the writer's mother?
. . . .

2 Explain in your own words why the author's mother ran the coffee shop.
. . . .

3 Why should a café of this kind be described as 'a good *pull-up* for car-men'
(including lorry drivers) (lines 6–7)? . . . .

4 Whom does the word 'we' in line 8 refer to? . . . .

5   What does the first sentence of the second paragraph imply about conditions at the time? . . . .

6   Why did the writer wonder why George Orwell 'made such a fuss' (line 13)? . . . .

7   'Unemployment was widespread' (line 13) can be expressed in different words as . . . .

8   A 'casual labourer' (line 15) is . . . .

9   'The remainder' (line 18) refers to . . . .

10   They 'drifted away' (line 18) suggests that . . . .

11   Why did the remainder (lines 18–19) go to the public library? . . . .

12   Why should Incubator Street (line 24) be a suitable name for a street swarming with children? . . . .

13   When might somebody be called 'underprivileged', line 26? . . . .

14   Why should the writer feel that he ought to ask permission to 'put aside false modesty' (lines 28–29)? . . . .

15   Explain in your own words the writer's attitude to his childhood surroundings. . . . .

16   Suggest the distinction between 'those who made news' and 'the true men of destiny' (lines 32–33). . . . .

17   Summarise in about 100 words why Shadwell was 'a grim place to grow up in' in the inter-war years. . . . .

Section C: Directed Writing
Suggestions and advice

Nature of this test

Together with the Paper 1 comprehension question, this exercise causes especial difficulty for many candidates, involving as it does various techniques which they may not be familiar with.

It is described in the examination syllabus as:

'a directed writing exercise to test ability to present information in a given form or style.'

The following types of possible exercises are suggested in the syllabus:

(a) a letter to which the candidate must compose a reply

(b) a table of figures of which the candidate must provide a written interpretation

(c) an extract from a report, or a list of notes, to be used as the basis of an article

(d) a newspaper article or an extract from a radio or television broadcast to be used as the basis of a formal letter to a newspaper

Other kinds of exercise involving the reproduction and transformation of given material may appear.

In all cases the information has to be produced or reproduced in a certain form or style: in many cases this involves a change from the form and/or style of the original.

The following abilities are essential in answering this question proficiently:
- (a) to understand and carry out the instructions exactly
- (b) to understand in detail whatever material is provided, and any possible implications
- (c) in many cases, to summarise
- (d) in certain cases, to provide additional related material
- (e) to recognise, from general experience of English, the kind of form and style intended
- (f) to produce the extracted and possibly supplemented information in the required form and style

Guidelines

1 Read the instructions slowly and with concentration, underlining or noting down exactly *what* you are asked to do (there may be several points to notice here) and *how* you must express your ideas. Bear in mind that changes will have to be made. This might involve:
- (a) presenting the information from a different, even the opposite point of view
- (b) drawing conclusions from or interpreting or explaining material
- (c) answering allegations or opinions
- (d) using only part of the information to support a certain case
- (e) presenting the material in a summarised or expanded form

In many cases you will be asked to supplement the material in some way, probably with your own ideas or opinions.

In all cases you will be expected to write in a given form or style.

Remember that any failure of your answer to conform to the instructions may result in the loss of a considerable number of marks.

2 Note especially any instruction on the number of words to be used in your answer.

3 Read the given material slowly and thoughtfully. Read it again with the instructions in mind.

4 Read the instructions again.

5 Decide the main topics or paragraph subjects you will be dealing with. It is unlikely that you will be able to present your material effectively in only one paragraph: two, three or possibly even four paragraphs may be needed. Marks will certainly be earned for intelligent planning.

6 Prepare your answer in rough by selecting, rearranging, interpreting and possibly summarising material from the data given. Additional material is considered and introduced at this stage: drawing conclusions, providing further examples, suggesting applications or objections, confirming with relevant facts etc. according to the instructions.

7 Check that the *arrangement, form* and *style* conform to the instructions. You may be asked to reproduce material in a more formal style. In this case, existing colloquial forms (slang, verbal abbreviations, incomplete sentences

53

and other features of conversation of the relaxed, highly personal or sensational style of the popular newspaper or magazine) would have to be converted into the more controlled and conventional style of formal writing. One difficulty will be finding suitable vocabulary to replace the more colloquial forms. Some of the other ways in which form, arrangement and style of the existing material might have to be transformed are suggested in exercises in this book.

8 Check the number of words used (as in the summary already dealt with on pages 43–44) and make any necessary modifications.

9 Copy the corrected answer into your examination answer book.

10 Read through what you have copied and correct where necessary.

Exercises

Model question and answer

The following story appeared in a local newspaper: '*The Canterhill Chronicle*'.

Write a letter to the London '*Times*' in which you refer to and make a brief summary of the story, and also express various reasons for your concern about the appalling risks that parents run when they leave young children alone in the house. Your style will probably be more formal than that of the local paper. The beginning of the letter has been written for you; write another 125–175 words.

Children rescued from blazing house
Parents celebrating pools win

Stephanie (aged 4) and Jonathan (aged 8) narrowly escaped appalling tragedy last Saturday evening when their home became a blazing inferno while their parents were in a pub half a mile away.

Timothy and Magda Clacton were at the 'Lucky Nugget' roadhouse celebrating a £200 win on the football pools, and knew nothing about their children's miraculous escape until they returned an hour later.

Magda was under sedation when our reporter called at her parents' house where the family are now staying, but Timothy told him, 'We never dreamt of anything like this happening. We'd heard about the pools win that morning and after the kids were in bed, we

slipped off to have a quick drink to celebrate it. Then we met some friends and we forgot about the time. We'd left the kids asleep. We never realised anything could happen to them.'

Now Jonathan admits he wasn't really asleep. 'I wanted to look at my picture-book,' he said, 'so I lit the candle and put it on the window-sill. Then I went to sleep. I think it got the curtains.'

Mr. Hereward Gabriel (aged 40), who happened to be passing, saw thick smoke coming out so he rang the front door bell. When he got no answer he climbed in a window and managed to carry the screaming children to safety. The house was almost completely destroyed.

Here is a beginning for your letter:

54

Sir,

A story I read in yesterday's 'Canterhill Chronicle' has caused me the gravest concern and as it clearly has widespread implications, I should like to bring it to the attention of your readers.

It is an account of...

Sir,

A story I read in yesterday's 'Canterhill Chronicle' has caused me the gravest concern and as it clearly has widespread implications, I should like to bring it to the attention of your readers.

It is an account of / the narrow escape from death of two young children left alone in their home while their parents were visiting a public house some distance away. The elder child, who was only eight, lit a candle which set light to the curtains, and the resulting fire destroyed the house, the children being saved only by the prompt and courageous action of a passer-by.

This is only one of many appalling fatalities which may occur during the absence of thoughtless parents. Warning children against danger is no safeguard: children are seldom aware of the consequences of their actions and the mere fact of being alone provides an opportunity for hazardous experiment. Playing with fire, knives and scissors, climbing, investigating dangerous electrical equipment are only some of the risks they may involve themselves in. Consider too the misery suffered by the nervous child left alone at night, longing for parental reassurance.

If only parents rash enough to take such risks had the imagination to realise the guilt and despair awaiting those who have returned home to disaster!

174 words

Practice exercises

First exercise

The Atmos Electrical and Radio Company employs around 800 workers. Recently there has been a good deal of dissatisfaction among employees, arising from problems connected with travel between their homes and place of work. The Company Personnel Manager, Miss Alison Northlind, has circulated a questionnaire to all employees to discover how they travel to and from work and what their problems are.

About three quarters of the staff returned a completed form and the information provided by their replies is summarised below. Miss Northlind is now preparing a report based on this information which she intends to present at the next meeting of the AERC Management Board. She concludes the report with one or two suggestions about steps that could be taken by the company to remedy some of the dissatisfaction felt.

Here is a summary of the information gathered:

Approximate numbers	Method of transport	Problems
250	Private car	Parking space provided for only 150 cars Little space available in surroundings
60	Motor-cycle or bicycle	Enough space and cycle racks provided but no protection from weather
90	Train	20-minute walk from station—no bus connection
130	Bus	Not enough buses and irregular service
60	On foot	—

The beginning of Miss Northlind's report has been written for you; complete it with between 125 and 175 words.

ATMOS ELECTRICAL AND RADIO COMPANY

Personnel Department   14th December, 19—

TRANSPORT AND RELATED FACILITIES FOR COMPANY STAFF

A questionnaire circulated last month among company staff and returned by 75% of the recipients has provided the following information about difficulties experienced by the Company's work force in travelling to and from work.

About 40% of those who answered come to work by private car
....

Second exercise

Most of the country of Saxanglia is undergoing the longest drought since records began, accompanied by record-breaking high temperatures. The newspaper headlines below refer to this occurrence and some of the results.

Write a formal report on the drought and its consequences to appear in the London 'Times'. Besides referring to the information supplied by the headlines, you should supply a few additional details which illustrate the facts given there. The items you regard as most important should come first.

NATIONWIDE DROUGHT LIKELY TO CONTINUE INDEFINITELY
DAIRY FARMERS PREDICT SERIOUS MILK SHORTAGE
FRUIT AND VEGETABLE PRICES SOAR
WATER RATIONING IN LARGE AREAS
WHERE HAVE ALL THE FLOWERS GONE?
BEER SHORTAGE THREATENED AS BREWERIES BROUGHT TO STANDSTILL

BAN ON CAR-WASHING AND GARDEN-SPRINKLERS
STRAWBERRY OR VANILLA—WHO CARES SO LONG AS IT'S
FROZEN?

The beginning of the report has been written for you. Write another 125 to 175 words.

The unprecedented drought which has been affecting Saxanglia shows no sign of breaking in the foreseeable future. No rain has fallen now for four months and abnormally high temperatures are making the situation more difficult.
Already ....

4 Listening comprehension

Suggestions and advice

Nature of this test

Three passages of about 300 words each are read aloud twice. There are five multiple-choice-type questions on each passage and answers to all five must be indicated.

Procedure

1   Each candidate is given two papers: a question paper, which has on it four sets of five multiple-choice items, and an answer sheet.
    The answer sheet has the numbers 1–20 on it, and each number is followed by the letters A, B, C and D. Instructions are shown as to how answers are to be recorded on this sheet. A pencil is used for recording answers and incorrect attempts can be rubbed out. This rubbing out must be done thoroughly as a sufficient impression of the wrong answer may remain and cause it to be read by the machine used in marking. Only 3 passages are given in each test. The examiner explains how the five numbers which apply to the unused test should be deleted.
2   The examiner explains how the answers are to be recorded and allows a minute to read through the questions (on the separate question paper) which apply to the first passage to be heard. (These may not relate to the first set of questions if the examiner has decided to leave out the first passage and present passages 2, 3 and 4.)
3   The passage already indicated is read through, and between 1 and 2 minutes are allowed for recording some of the answers.
4   The same passage is read a second time and again 1–2 minutes are allowed, this time for completing the answers.
5   The examiner indicates the next group of questions to be dealt with and allows about 1 minute for reading these through.
6   The other passages chosen by the examiner are presented in turn and are dealt with in the same way as the first.

The aim of this part of the examination is to test the candidate's ability to under-stand what is heard, not only in general terms but in some detail, and to apply this understanding to the given responses. The questions are normally less demanding than those related to Reading comprehension, with less call for minute concentration on detail, but they may test whether a relatively small point or a certain development of ideas has been noticed and interpreted correctly.

Guidelines

1 Read the questions indicated by the examiner very carefully. They may mean little to you before you have heard the passage, but certain clues about what to expect and listen for particularly will be there.

Example: What type of employee was the firm looking for?
A Highly-qualified students just leaving university.
B Young people with practical experience.
C Young employees who had successfully completed technical college courses.
D Workers who had recently completed apprenticeships.

Consideration of these possibilities should indicate the particular point you will be listening for.

2 Listen carefully to the first reading. Your primary objective is to understand the general subject matter and development of the passage, though you may notice the answers to the questions you have in mind. It is almost certainly not a good idea to indicate these answers during the reading as this will interrupt concentration: you may miss an important point and misinterpret the rest of the passage as a result.

3 After the first hearing, read all the questions again in the light of the information you now have. Record those answers you are quite sure of. Make sure you will remember the unanswered questions during the final reading. You may already have some ideas about them which you will be able to check.

4 You should now know exactly what you are going to give special attention to while listening to the second reading. Try also to confirm the correctness of the answers already indicated.

5 Use the last moments for recording the final answers and checking. If you are sure no changes need be made, you could start considering the questions on the next passage.
You will have a few spare moments before giving the papers in, so you could leave single undecided answers for a final quick consideration then.

(The passages on which the following questions are based are to be found in the Key to this book, which is published separately.)

Questions and responses

You will hear each passage read twice over, and you will be given time to choose your answers to the questions on each passage. Write the number of each ques-

tion and after it the letter A, B, C or D for the answer you choose. *Give one
answer only* to each question.

First passage

1 One feature of the Christmas tree was that

    A it was decorated with glass balls of various colours
    B it had a golden star on the top
    C the presents would be in golden boxes under the tree
    D there were different sizes of glass balls

2 The children referred to

    A were Hilary's own
    B were not necessarily related to one another
    C were Uncle Flea's nephews and nieces
    D were helping Uncle Flea with the presents

3 Uncle Flea's job was to

    A deliver the presents
    B distribute the presents
    C provide the presents
    D carry the presents into the house

4 What was Uncle Flea's other name?

    A Vincent
    B Troy
    C Forrester
    D the name is not mentioned in the passage

5 Troy appeared to think Hilary's suggestion about the gloves was

    A useful
    B impossible
    C pointless
    D unwise

6 What was Hilary's opinion of a sprinkling of snow?

    A He welcomed the idea
    B It would not be advisable because of the old man's poor health
    C It would not last very long
    D It would run on to the carpet

Second passage

1 What aspect of a storm are we told about in the first few sentences?

    A Its danger
    B Its effects
    C An explanation of a storm
    D What happens in a storm

2 How is it possible to estimate the distance away that the centre of a thunderstorm is?

    A From how quickly the lightning follows the thunder
    B From the period between the lightning and the thunder
    C From the type of lightning that can be seen
    D From the length of time between the claps of thunder

3 When could lightning conductors first be developed?

    A As soon as the necessary materials became available
    B When people understood what lightning was
    C As soon as people realised the need for them
    D When it was realised that this was not very difficult

4 Which of the following is the safest place to be in a storm?

    A In the open air
    B In a valley
    C Near a wall
    D Underground

5 Why is it dangerous to shelter under trees in a thunderstorm?

    A Lightning might strike the person and not the tree
    B Electricity may be diverted from the tree to the person near it
    C Being good conductors, trees are often struck by lightning
    D They give a false impression of safety

6 Why can wire fences be dangerous to human beings?

    A They can store powerful electric charges
    B They may conduct and discharge electrical currents
    C Current carried along becomes increasingly powerful
    D Lightning is more likely to strike in areas near a wire fence

7 Some people are particularly unpleasantly affected by thunderstorms because

    A physical changes in their bodies stimulate feelings of terror
    B they are terrified by the effect the storm has upon their bodies
    C their fear causes certain physical reactions
    D an increasing terror of the danger involved makes them lose their nerve completely

Third passage

1 Where was the boat when Jensen first demanded to be put ashore?

    A Moving alongside the river bank
    B Approaching Tower Bridge
    C On the far side of Tower Bridge
    D Passing under Tower Bridge

2　What could be seen on either side as the boat moved down river?

    A　The lights of London
    B　A high river bank
    C　A line of buildings
    D　A row of high shops

3　What did Gansert want to do with Jensen?

    A　Prevent him by all means from escaping
    B　Convince him that it was advisable to stay on the ship
    C　Make him afraid of what would happen to him if he left the ship
    D　Frighten him into remaining on board

4　Gansert's feeling of elation (enjoyable excitement) was due to the fact that

    A　he had managed to kidnap his enemy Jensen
    B　his plan had been successful
    C　his enemy was now in his power
    D　there was now a chance of discovering much-needed information

5　Jensen's second attempt to be put ashore differed from his first in that

    A　he now seemed somewhat nervous
    B　he was now begging for what he wanted
    C　he was making a request, not giving a command
    D　he now did not really want to go ashore

Fourth passage

1　Why did the group of people go to live in the White House?

    A　They were looking for adventure
    B　They were a group of friends who wanted to live together
    C　They believed in working together and sharing things
    D　Having no plans for the future, they decided on this as an experiment

2　What was their first problem?

    A　There were not enough rooms for them all
    B　There was some bitterness about the occupation of the rooms
    C　There was a certain dissatisfaction about the standard of rooms available
    D　They could not agree about which rooms were the best

3　What arrangements were made about the cooking?

    A　Men and women usually cooked together
    B　Meals were prepared by everybody working together
    C　They all cooked their own food
    D　Everybody took a turn at cooking

4　The result of the arrangement for cooking was that

    A　the standard of cooking varied considerably
    B　they were able to enjoy international menus each day

C the variety of food caused indigestion

D they enjoyed the advantage of trying out some strange new dishes

5 What did the writer discover about the drinks available?

A These sometimes reflected other people's unwelcome ideas

B Some of them had a bad effect on his health

C Genuine coffee was not served for health reasons

D He always found the drinks unpleasant

6 The overall impression of the White House given by the passage is that

A the inmates were living in primitive conditions

B there was constant grumbling and quarrelling

C they all worked very hard

D there was little attempt at organisation

5 Interview

General Procedure

1 The candidate is allowed about 15 minutes before actually meeting the examiner to prepare a talk on a selected topic and also to read aloud from a dialogue. He is handed a paper on which three topics are shown, of which he has to choose one to talk about, and a dialogue where he will read one part and the examiner will read the other.

2 Shortly before he goes to meet the examiner, he is usually given a slip of paper showing his name and examination number: this he gives to the examiner on entering.

3 The interview is in four parts: a conversation about a photograph, a two-minute talk by the candidate on his chosen topic, reading aloud, and responses to three situations. The four parts can be dealt with in any order at the examiner's discretion, but the order suggested here is probably the most common one.

Section A: Conversation based on the scene or action shown in a photograph
Suggestions and advice

Nature of this test

About 5 minutes are given to this section.

A photograph is handed to the candidate, who is given a few seconds to look at it. A conversation follows, the first part of which, (*a*) is concerned with the picture itself, and the second (*b*) with a discussion of topics related to the picture.

(*a*) Some aspects of the photograph which may be discussed are:

(i) information about objects and people shown there

Examples: Describe the man on the left.

There are three different groups of people in the picture—what is each group doing?

How can you tell that the road shown is a motorway?

(ii) implications drawn from the picture

Examples: Why do you think the man on the right looks impatient?

What indications suggest that this photograph was taken in summer?

(*b*) This involves a discussion between examiner and candidate of opinions and ideas about general topics related in some way to the photograph. For example, a picture of a motorway may lead to a discussion of present-day traffic problems; that of an office to ideas about different kinds of jobs and their advantages and drawbacks, or an expression of the candidate's opinion of office work.

Aim of this test

Primarily this is to discover the candidate's ability to take part in a conversation on an unprepared subject.

The originality or value of the ideas is not so important, though the candidate must be able to respond to the question and have something useful to say that is relevant to the subject.

The examiner is most interested in the following:

1   comprehension of the question or other remarks made by the examiner
2   the ability to converse on the subject (*a*) relevantly (*b*) suitably (*c*) fluently (*d*) with an effective vocabulary (*e*) with correct and varied structural forms
3   absence of mistakes
4   an adequate standard of pronunciation and intonation.

Standards of Assessment

General consideration

One of the original purposes of the Proficiency examination was to test a student's ability to benefit from a course in English at a British university.

This would involve not merely an ability to understand lectures and to read books at an advanced level but also to write essays, make notes, answer questions in written and oral examinations, and take an active part in group study and discussions. Assessment of all papers, not only Interview standards, is still partially related to the above requirements and a good pass reflects an ability to follow successfully British university courses in subjects which students are qualified to undertake at this level.

Achievement in the spoken language

In the light of the above considerations the candidate should have the ability

1   to understand, without difficulty or hesitation, conversation not only on everyday topics but also on such general issues as are discussed in newspapers and on the radio. While the language used would not be unduly formal or

colloquial, it would not normally be simplified from the accustomed speech of an educated British person.

2 to respond suitably and have something useful to say.

3 to have a wide range of vocabulary put to active use, familiarity with common idioms, facility with a variety of more advanced structural forms, and considerable fluency.

4 to have a pronunciation that can be easily understood and is not strikingly foreign, though the standard may well be rather lower than that achieved when reading aloud.

Guidelines

1 Almost all candidates feel nervous and the examiner knows this, sympathises and makes allowances. Remember the examiner is human, has met many other nervous candidates and has probably been a nervous candidate himself in oral tests and interviews.

2 Listen with concentration. If you are not sure you have understood, you can ask, 'Would you mind saying that again?' or 'Could you explain the meaning of the word "——"?' If you fail completely to understand, you can make the request, 'I'm not sure that I understood. Could you say that in another way perhaps?' Obviously, you should not do this too often!

3 Be careful to answer the question that has been asked. You can add ideas but these ought to be relevant to the question.

4 Avoid rushing into an answer before you have thought what you are going to say. The expression on your face will probably show you have understood while you are considering for some four or five seconds how to frame a suitable answer.

5 The purpose of this test is to discover how effectively you can express yourself, so avoid the single-word answer. Even in cases where a limited 'yes' or 'no' is appropriate, go on from there to give reasons and/or extra ideas.

6 Speak clearly and loudly enough to be heard easily.

7 Do not hurry. Speaking quickly does not indicate proficiency in speaking, and may well result in a variety of faults, including the following:

(a) the examiner may have difficulty in understanding you

(b) you may lose the thread of what you are trying to say

(c) you may wander from the point

(d) unnecessary mistakes in grammar and structure are far more likely

Speak at a moderate speed, planning the effective expression of your ideas as you go.

8 At Proficiency level you are being tested not merely on your ability to answer in correct English but also on your full command of the language. As you speak, try to devise ways of using the passive vocabulary and structures stored in your mind. (Further advice is given later about pre-examination practice.) Slang and fashionable expressions should be viewed with distrust, especially if you have not lived in England for some time. Used in the wrong

context, they can sound odd and forced.

Here is an example of a pleasant, easy-going but controlled and informed manner of speaking:

An opinion on national standards of cooking

This is something that nobody can judge really objectively. We've all got our own prejudices based on tastes developed in childhood. I suppose good marks can be earned for the interest in cooking the average person has, and the time and trouble given to preparing interesting meals. But fashion and food snobbery play a large part in forming people's opinions.

9 As you are speaking, you are very likely to realise you have made a mistake. Stop and correct it quickly and then continue.

  'We probably experience the same problems in our country like you do in ... sorry: as you do in yours.'

Pre-examination preparation

The ability to express ideas fluently depends largely on the time you can give to practising this. This practice can be carried out when you are alone as well as in class. Here are two among several possibilities:

 (*a*) Read through an English passage and then ask yourself and answer (in English) questions on it.

 (*b*) Similar self-questions and answers can be based on a picture, though in this case you have not the help of the vocabulary in a passage.

Both these exercises can be practised with a friend.

Develop the habit of an internal English monologue: about things noticed while you are waiting for a bus, people seen in a train, things that have happened during the day.

Photographs

Photograph 1

Suggested range of questions and topics

1 Contrast the three people you can see in the photograph.

2 Why might many people find this an appealing or attractive picture?

3 What is the baby's apparent attitude to the doctor?

4 What things suggest that the mother is both proud and also fond of her baby?

How the father, family and friends usually behave after the arrival of a baby, especially a first child.

Describe the ideal doctor.

Why you would or would not like to be a doctor.

State provision of hospital and medical care in your country.

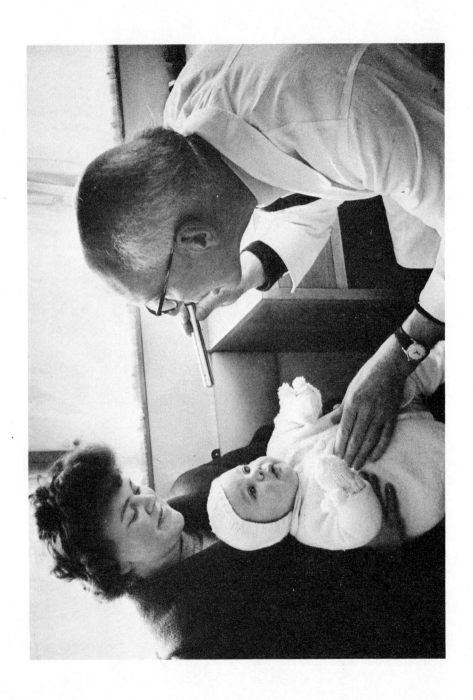

Photograph 2

Suggested range of questions and topics

1 Describe the differences between the boy and the girl in clothing, facial expression and appearance.

2 What has each of them been doing during the past few minutes?

3 What things suggest that their task is almost completed?

One job in a kitchen you enjoy doing, one you don't mind doing and one you hate doing.

To what extent is the kitchen the most important room in the house?

Your opinion of the idea that it lowers a man's dignity to work or help in the kitchen.

An ideal kitchen.

Should boys and girls be brought up to share equally in helping their parents with domestic jobs?

Photograph 3

Suggested range of questions and topics

1 In what various ways have the two people made themselves comfortable in their home?

2 Why does the man in particular look relaxed and comfortable?

3 Suggest some differences between this sitting-room and your own, or a typical sitting-room in your country.

4 What things suggest that the newspaper you can see is not of a particularly intellectual type?

'Many ordinary people of today enjoy greater comfort and security than great kings of the past'. In what ways is this statement true?

Some of the advantages middle-aged and elderly people may have over younger ones.

Ways of lighting homes through the centuries.

Some of the possible benefits of television.

73

Section B: A talk on a topic
Suggestions and advice

Nature of this test

The talk should last about two minutes.

A sheet with a reading passage (dialogue) and three topics on it is handed to each candidate 15 minutes before the interview starts.

One topic is chosen by the candidate, who is allowed to make notes on another piece of paper but not to write a complete answer. During the interview the candidate is allowed to refer to the notes but not read straight from the paper. He must face and speak directly to the examiner, glancing down at the notes from time to time if this is necessary.

Aim of this test

This is a test of the candidate's ability to communicate orally at length in an organised fashion: it is the equivalent of making a short uninterrupted speech.

Standards of Assessment

Material presented

Marks are given for the relevance and arrangement of the material. Strictly speaking, qualities such as a wide knowledge of the subject, originality, humour, the ability to speak entertainingly can hardly attract additional marks in the limited context of a short talk, though they obviously make a pleasant impression on the examiner.

Language ability

As in the case of the photograph-based conversation, a Proficiency candidate is expected to be fluent and able to make use of a wide vocabulary and range of structures, and to have an ability to vary sentence length and complexity.

Correctness

Even fewer mistakes should appear than in the conversation as there has been some preparation, and the candidate can concentrate on what is being said without the necessity of understanding and adapting to the examiner's questions.

Guidelines

1   The 15-minute interval allowed for preparation has to cover consideration both of the topic and the dialogue, so you will have to decide how much time to allot to each. One possibility is to divide your time as follows:

5 minutes: choice of topic and decision about method of approach and main points (which you jot down).

5 minutes: dialogue preparation.

5 minutes: return to the topic (you may be surprised at the many new ideas that have come into your mind in the interval). Decide what details you are going to deal with as part of each main point. You may also think of some effective expressions you can make use of.

2 The two minutes allowed for the talk may seem to pass much more quickly than you anticipate (compare this with the 60 minutes spent on an essay, even allowing for the extra time spent on writing). However, it is clearly better to have rather too much material ready than too little.

3 It must be quite clear that you have planned your talk—with two or three subjects considered in logical order (similar to composition preparation).

List the main subjects with a few ideas to develop under each. You may be dealing with a topic that whole books have been written about, so selection of ideas and/or the choice of a certain type of approach is important. Here is an example of pre-interview notes. The topic is 'Caravans'.

Five headings are suggested but the first and last can be dealt with in very few words.

(*a*) Introduction: basic idea—living while moving.

(*b*) Desert caravan: traders moving together—safety in deserts and other wild places; accommodation could be tents pitched nightly.

(*c*) Gipsy caravans: change in word meaning—now signifies a moving home; gipsy caravans can be comfortable permanent homes; may be drawn by horse or remain stationary for a long time.

(*d*) Holiday caravans: mobility + temporary home; all shapes and sizes with basic living necessities; now an extra—used for enjoyment; development of stationary caravan sites—sometimes caravan used as permanent home.

(*e*) Romantic impression people have of past though not of present-day caravans.

Try to give your talk something of the shape of a composition, with a suitable beginning and ending.

4 Make the most of your language resources when speaking.

5 Speak clearly and at a reasonable, measured speed. Try to give an impression of a confidence you may not actually be feeling!

6 Other suggestions relating to the conversation based on the photograph are valid here also, including the self-correcting of mistakes. No marks are lost if you go back and correct the mistake or rephrase the sentence sensibly and calmly.

Pre-examination preparation

This is easier to practise alone than the conversation about the photograph. You can find possible topics in this book or think of them for yourself. Prepare notes and then talk about them, stopping to improve what you have said whenever you can. As the examination approaches, practise working on the topic and the dialogue in the allotted 15 minutes.

Topics

Prepare yourself to speak for 2 minutes on any *one* of the following topics. You may make notes on a separate piece of paper and refer to them during your talk, but you must not write out the complete talk and simply read it aloud.

1 The advantages and drawbacks of living in a very large city.
2 The kinds of noises which are most likely to get on your nerves. Try to explain why this is likely to happen.
3 Has a doctor, an ambulance driver, a policeman or any other person whose services may be urgently needed the right to strike to achieve better conditions for himself/herself?

Section C: Reading aloud of a dialogue
Suggestions and advice

Nature of this test

This will take 2–3 minutes.
A short extract from a play on the same sheet as the Topic is given to the candidate 15 minutes before the Interview starts. One of the parts, the longer of the two, is read by the candidate, the other by the examiner.
It is necessary, therefore, not only to achieve good pronunciation but also, by the use of suitable intonation patterns, emphasis and pauses, to adapt reasonably to the character who is supposed to be speaking the given part.

Standards of assessment

A good mark depends on proficiency in the following:
  (*a*) correct sounds: vowels, diphthongs, consonants
  (*b*) correct stress in individual words
  (*c*) the use of weakened forms where appropriate, and a knowledge of when to weaken a word in context and when to give it its full vowel value
  (*d*) catenation—linking together words in a word group and transferring a final consonant to a following word starting with a vowel
  (*e*) rhythm and stress as related to words in context
  (*f*) intonation patterning

(g) emphasis of separate words and of word groups in conveying meaning and/or feeling

(h) pauses to create certain effects.

These various aspects of pronunciation cannot be marked individually, but each one influences the general impression on which the mark is based.

Certain obvious weaknesses would in themselves, however, result in loss of marks. These include especially:

(a) consistent sound faults—in vowels, diphthongs and consonants

(b) incorrect word stress, such as a constant stress on the final syllable

(c) constant use of strong forms in place of weakened ones e.g. the indefinite article, prepositions such as *of* and *for*, weakened forms of the verb *to be*

(d) absence or unnaturalness of intonation.

The examination syllabus states:

'The main emphasis in the assessment will be on pronunciation factors, including stress, intonation and rhythm, and appropriate forms.

Guidelines

Pre-examination preparation

(a) The basic theory of effective reading aloud should be familiar, including accepted sound values, when and how to weaken words or syllables and the significance and nature of intonation patterns. Regular guided practice should have been carried out.

(b) If you have a native English-speaking teacher, listen critically to all these aspects of speaking, giving special attention to intonation and how this is used to produce certain effects of meaning and feeling.

Listen to B.B.C. programmes (B.B.C. Overseas Service on short waves— you can obtain particulars of programmes and wave-lengths from the B.B.C. in London) or to records of British speakers. So far as pronunciation and intonation are concerned, even elementary language records can be useful.

(c) Practice reading aloud even when you are alone. Concentrate on single sentences, paying special attention to single features such as sounds you have difficulty with, word stress, weakening and intonation patterns. Practise until the improved form becomes automatic. Remember however that without a model and/or critic there will still be mistakes you yourself cannot detect, and there is a danger of reinforcing these.

(d) Try to persuade a native English speaker who speaks the kind of English that sounds acceptable to you to record some passages on tape in separate short groups. You can then work on these passages alone before submitting them to criticism. Try to develop a critical ability which can distinguish between your own recording and that of your model.

Be conscious of your pronunciation, especially your weaknesses, and aim at improvement all the time. Many students are too easily contented with their standard.

Preparation of the examination passage

Pay special attention to your known difficulties as you examine the part you are asked to read and, although you are not allowed to mark the paper, make a mental note of them. Provided this cannot be heard by any other candidate, you can whisper words and word groups that need concentrated practice. Consider the feelings, implications and special meanings being expressed, and how to show these by means of intonation, emphasis and pauses.

The examination

Read to the examiner at a natural speed: on no account rush through your part. Reading that is rather too slow will make a better impression than a rapid gabble. Clear, completely audible speaking is essential.

Dialogues

Dialogue 1

Prepare yourself to read the part of MRS. DUBEDAT.

Ridgeon: I mean the gentleman that dined with us: an excellent and honest man, whose life is as valuable as anyone else's. I have arranged that I shall take his case, and that Sir Ralph Bloomfield Bonington shall take Mr. Dubedat's.

MRS. DUBEDAT: I see what it is. Oh! it is envious, mean, cruel. And I thought that you would be above such a thing.

Ridgeon: What do you mean?

MRS. DUBEDAT: Oh, do you think I don't know? Do you think it has never happened before? Why does everybody turn against him? Can you not forgive him for being superior to you? for being cleverer? for being braver? for being a great artist?

Ridgeon: Yes: I can forgive him all that.

MRS. DUBEDAT: Well, have you anything to say against him? I have challenged everyone who has turned against him— challenged them face to face to tell me any wrong thing he has done, any ignoble thought he has uttered. They have always confessed that they could not tell me one. I challenge you now. What do you accuse him of?

Ridgeon: I am like all the rest. Face to face, I cannot tell you one thing against him.

MRS. DUBEDAT: But your manner is changed. And you have broken your promise to me to make room for him as your patient.

Ridgeon: I think you are a little unreasonable. You have had the very best medical advice in London for him; and his case has

78

	been taken in hand by a leader of the profession. Surely—
MRS. DUBEDAT:	Oh, it is so cruel to keep telling me that. It seems all right; and it puts me in the wrong. But I am not in the wrong. I have faith in you and I have no faith in the others. We have seen so many doctors: I have come to know at last when they are only talking and can do nothing. It is different with you. I feel that you know. You must listen to me, doctor. Oh, will you please sit down and listen to me just for a few minutes. Thank you. I won't keep you long; but I must tell you the whole truth. Listen. I know Louis as nobody else in the world knows him or ever can know him. I am his wife. I know he has little faults: impatience, sensitiveness, even little selfishnesses that are too trivial for him to notice. I know that he sometimes shocks people about money because he is so utterly above it, and can't understand the value ordinary people set on it. Tell me: did he—did he borrow any money from you.
Ridgeon:	He asked me for some—once.
MRS. DUBEDAT:	Oh, I am so sorry—so sorry. But he will never do it again: I pledge you my word for that. He has given me his promise: here in this room just before you came; and he is incapable of breaking his word. That was his only real weakness; and now it is conquered and done with for ever.

Dialogue 2

Prepare yourself to read the part of MISS MOFFAT.

Morgan:	But you ... will be staying here ... how can I never come back—after everything you have done for me?
MISS MOFFAT:	Do you remember, the last six months, I've gone for a long walk over the moors, every morning at eight, like clockwork, for my health?
Morgan:	Yes?
MISS MOFFAT:	There's one bit of the road, round a boulder—and there's an oak tree, and under it the valley suddenly drops sheer. Every morning regularly, as I was turning that corner, by some trick of the mind, I found myself thinking of you working for this scholarship, and winning it. And I experienced something which must after all be comparatively rare: a feeling ... of complete happiness. I shall experience it again. No, Morgan Evans, you have no duty to me. Your only duty—is to the world.
Morgan:	To the world?

MISS MOFFAT:	Now you are going, there is no harm in telling you something. I don't think you realise quite how exceptional you are, or what your future can become if you give it the chance. I have always been very definite about the things I wanted, and I have always had everything worked out to a T—perhaps that's the trouble with me, I don't know ... I've got you worked out, and it's up to you whether it will come right or not.
Morgan:	Go on.
MISS MOFFAT:	I rather made out to the Squire that I wanted you to be a writer—the truth might have sounded ridiculous; but stranger things have happened. You have brains, shrewdness, eloquence, imagination and enough personality; and Oxford will give you enough of the graces.
Morgan:	For what?
MISS MOFFAT:	Enough to become a great statesman of our country. It needn't be just politics—it could be more, much, much more—it could be ... for a future nation to be proud of.... Perhaps I'm mad, I don't know. We'll see. I know you're absurdly young for such an idea, and that so far you've only got the groundwork—I know all that; but I've got the measure of your intellect better than you have yourself. It's up to you....

Section D: Situations
Suggestions and advice

Nature of this test

This part of the Interview will last about 2–3 minutes.
During the Interview, the candidate is given a paper listing a number of situations. The examiner then reads aloud, one at a time, three of the situations. The candidate has to express exactly what he or she would say if faced by the situation in question. A few moments are allowed for consideration.

Standards of assessment

(a) The candidate must clearly understand the situation and how to respond effectively and suitably.

(b) The examination syllabus suggests that the candidate should make an appropriate response, paying due attention to tone and manner and the use of socially acceptable forms—that is to say, the conventional way of expressing greeting, a complaint, congratulations, regret, a request, warning, and other responses appropriate to a situation.

(c) The response should be as free as possible from grammatical, structural and other errors.

(d) Responses to situations form part of the First Certificate Interview. The range of situations at Proficiency level will be wider, possibly including some that require considerable tact and skilful handling, and standards of expression and correctness will also be very much higher.

The main difficulty involved in this test

As a linguistic exercise the test need not involve many problems, so long as the candidate is thoroughly familiar with a wide range of socially acceptable language forms which can be adapted to the various situations and the particular impression that the speaker wishes to create with his words.

However, social responses in Britain may in themselves differ from those approved in various other countries: certain British responses may seem abrupt, inconsiderate or too blunt; others may appear too humble, smooth and even servile.

The following situation might be dealt with differently in various countries.

Example: As a very junior employee you have to correct a statement made by somebody in a position of considerable authority.

(In a case like this, try to devise a possible statement to contradict)

Response: Excuse me, sir. The figures you've just quoted—do they in fact apply to last month? I understood that we had a balance of £2,500,000 then.

(Suitable intonation would be very important in this response)

This kind of response is difficult as it may involve considerable experience in social relationships, in avoiding giving offence and hurting feelings for example. Allowance is made for this and you will probably earn a satisfactory mark if you use reasonably suitable forms.

Guidelines

1 Pre-examination preparation: be familiar with and practise in many contexts the various forms of conventional politeness (e.g. 'I wonder if you'd mind . . .' 'Do you think you could . . .' 'I'm afraid I'm not at all satisfied with . . .' etc.) Practise responses to the situations listed in this book and devise some more of your own. A useful guideline is to put yourself in the place of the person you must address: will he be angry, hurt, offended, non-co-operative? How can you put across your request politely but firmly so as to secure co-operation or assistance?

(Some suggested responses are shown in the Key to this book)

2 Concentrate on the implications of the situation as the examiner reads it and you read it after to yourself, and *take time*—several seconds—before answering. *Do not rush into an answer* and find yourself stuck in a false situation or a muddled sentence halfway through.

3 You have to express what you would *say* in the given situation, not what you would do.

4   Make full use of the forms of conventional politeness you have learned.
5   You are more likely to avoid making grammatical and structural mistakes if you plan your answer beforehand. Do not hesitate to correct a mistake or rephrase an incorrect or clumsy sentence when necessary—this does not result in a loss of marks.
6   Keep to the point. Your answer should be effective and short.

Situations

1   You want to enrol for a Proficiency English course in a school or college and are asked about the extent of your knowledge of English. What do you say?
2   You have applied to an agency which arranges au pair jobs in Britain and have been asked to explain in English the kinds of jobs in the home you would be prepared to do. What do you say?
3   When asked for your railway ticket you cannot find it though you certainly had one. Explain to the ticket collector.
4   You want to consult a doctor but when you get to his surgery, you find the waiting-room full of people. For some urgent reason you must leave in at most half an hour. Explain the matter to the receptionist and try to persuade her to allow you to see the doctor before your turn.
5   You are attending a summer school in Britain and have paid to stay with a local family. The accommodation proves to be unsatisfactory in several ways. Explain to the course director why you want to change.
6   You have bought tickets for a theatre performance on a certain evening but find you cannot attend then. Explain this to the box office attendant and ask whether your tickets can be exchanged for another performance on a date and at a time which you suggest.
7   You are waiting at the Airport for your luggage to be delivered for examination by Customs, and all your fellow-passengers have already been dealt with. Inform an official of the non-appearance of your luggage, giving the necessary details about the luggage itself and the flight you came on.
8   You want to rent a small flat and so you call at an agency. Describe the kind of flat you would like to find.
9   Your teenage son or daughter is attending a summer school course in Britain. He/she has promised to write on arrival but after ten days you have still heard nothing. What do you say when you telephone the secretary of the course?
10 On your return from a wonderful holiday you are asked by a friend how you enjoyed it. You know the friend would love to have had such a holiday but family responsibilities have not allowed any holiday at all. Without actually lying, give a less than favourable impression of your experience.

Stage 2

Intermediate Level

1 Composition

Section A: Subjects for Composition

Narrative

1 You have to attend an important selection interview for a job you would very much like to get. There are several people on the interviewing committee and your experience is an unnerving one. Write about the interview, showing how the circumstances, surroundings, people on the committee and their behaviour have a slightly nightmarish quality.

2 Before starting serious preparation for a career, you decided to spend a period of six months to a year gaining a wider experience of life and people and, to some extent, getting to know and testing yourself. Relate what you did, your experience and discoveries.

3 A normally calm and easy-going person on one occasion loses his/her temper and even to some extent self-control. Give some details of the person involved, the background and circumstances leading up to the outburst and the effect it had on those present and on the person in question.

4 After a number of lessons you decided to take a driving test but this proved to be a near-disaster. Tell the story of what happened from the time you made your decision, filling in details of the circumstances in which the test drive was carried out, the examiner, the drive itself and the sequel.

Description

1 Describe some kind of small town or suburban Social Centre in which local residents, including old people, can come together for meetings, entertainment and companionship.

2 Describe the kind of person you consider to be the ideal mother *or* teacher *or* sportsman (or sportswoman) *or* politician.

3 Describe a student demonstration or some other demonstration which took the form of a march through the town centre. Relate briefly the cause of the demonstration and the preparations, but most of your composition should seek to give an impression of some of the people taking part, the onlookers' reactions and your own feelings as a participant or spectator.

4   Describe the same person at twenty, at forty and at sixty years of age, indicating how, while certain features of appearance, behaviour and character change, others remain fairly constant.

5   You have been visiting a museum of applied art in which there are old and more modern objects of pottery, metalware, glass and ivory, manuscripts, jewellery and embroidery. Two quite different objects remain in your memory afterwards. Describe these.

Facts and opinion

1   What would you hope to gain (or have already gained) from a period of study at a university?

2   What features of their home-life may assist in moulding anti-social young people?

3   Write a short account of two types of 'supernatural' manifestation, such as ghostly appearances, messages from spirits, omens, clairvoyance (seeing the future) or other phenomena not yet explained by science, indicating in each case your own attitude to the subject and possible explanations.

4   Our responsibility towards animals and all living creatures other than human beings.

5   Suggest three books of contrasting types which you would enjoy re-reading many times, and justify your high opinion of each of them.

6   You are the fairly conventional parent of a fourteen-year-old boy or girl who is restless, bored, resentful of authority, impulsive and easily influenced by people of a similar type. You live in a large town. What would be some of the things you might worry about when considering your child's immediate and future development?

7   What possible effects do you think that extensive television viewing may have on children below the age of sixteen?

8   What do you regard as the value and ideals of sport? How far are such values a feature of international sports contests?

Section B: Passages for Comprehension

Read the following passages and then answer the questions which follow them.

Model questions and answers

They're making it safer now for shoppers. Traffic is being banished from roads once crowded with vehicles. Spacious tree-lined areas are being set aside so that even the most absent-minded pedestrian can stroll about without danger to life and limb.

5   But can they? I'd say these areas are about as safe as minefields, and a shopper needs to be both nimble and alert to survive a trip through them.

Easily the most lethal hazard is the baby perambulator. Determined mothers propelling beautiful but belligerent-looking babies in these war chariots force their way through crowds like tanks. Step smartly out of their path or receive their glare of reprimand.

One resourceful mother actually wrote to a newspaper telling other pram pushers how to deal with slow movers. 'Put a bell on your pram handle,' she advised. 'Ring it sharply and you'll find going through crowds easy.'

What fiend invented the wheeled shopping trolley? Handled skilfully one of these is capable of a ruthless, three-pronged attack. Strategically placed behind one they are a most efficient tripping device. Wheeled over toes they can cripple for the day, and the cruel brake spike can almost amputate a foot at the ankle. A few nimble old ladies armed with these formidable weapons, sent in V formation into a rioting crowd, would be more efficient than a squad of mounted police.

Other treacherous dangers abound. Dog leads that trip the unwary. Little doggies trained to dive under one's feet, then to whine pathetically. Packs of larger dogs such as Doberman Pinschers, Alsatians and St. Bernards are all nicely groomed and taken for Saturday walkies, not into the countryside, but on to busy city streets.

A sharp look-out is needed also for the man with the walking cane. Some oldsters wield a pretty deadly stick, and pepper the pavements and anyone on them with stabs more destructive than a hail of rubber bullets.

Bricks were hurled at the brave souls who first ventured out in public carrying umbrellas. I'm not suggesting a return to such extreme tactics, but would earnestly plead: bring back the sou'wester and oilskin, so no one runs the risk of being blinded while out shopping through a 'safe' precinct.

These will be really safe only when all wheeled vehicles are banned from them, and when the police are allowed to frisk the public and remove dangerous weapons as they do with the soccer lads.[1]

(a) Explain the connection between the main idea being developed in each of the first two paragraphs.

While the first paragraph expresses the accepted belief that the new traffic-free shopping areas are much safer for all pedestrians, the second, in contrast, asserts that they are exceedingly dangerous.

(b) Why must the shopper need to be both 'nimble' and 'alert' (l. 6)?

He must be alert to the hidden but approaching danger and nimble or quick-moving in avoiding it.

(c) Quote three expressions from the third paragraph with which the writer gives a clear idea of the aggressiveness of perambulators and their occupants.

(i) belligerent-looking babies (ii) war chariots (iii) like tanks

[1] soccer lads = football hooligans

(*d*) In what way was the mother described in line 11 resourceful?

She had devised her own effective method of dealing with what was for her an obstacle.

(*e*) Why should it have been a 'fiend' (l. 14) who invented the wheeled shopping trolley?

A fiend is a devil, in this case someone who devises evil and destructive things like the dangerous wheeled shopping trolley.

(*f*) How does the writer illustrate the offensive power of the wheeled shopping trolley by her reference to the effective action of the old ladies mentioned in lines 18–20?

The wheeled shopping trolley is so efficient and ruthless in attack that, armed with it, even old ladies could do more to disperse rioters than a highly-trained body of mounted police.

(*g*) Comment on the writer's use of the word 'doggies' for 'dog' in line 22.

The writer is using the word ironically. 'Doggie' is a small child's name for a dog and suggests a sweet little helpless pet who 'whines pathetically' after deliberately diving under a person's foot. The person innocently involved may have fallen and hurt himself considerably, but everybody's sympathy is with the poor little animal who caused the trouble.

(*h*) Comment on the use of the word 'pepper' (l. 27) for the way in which the 'oldsters' (l. 27) use their sticks.

The top of a pepper pot is normally perforated with small holes through which the pepper is sprinkled. The pavements and the feet of the passers-by presumably have similar small holes left in them by the stabs of the old men's sticks.

(*i*) Suggest two ways in which the end of the passage gives the impression that the writer does not intend or expect to have the claims she has made taken too seriously.

The idea of the police inspecting the public, confiscating walking sticks and umbrellas and forbidding mothers to wheel perambulators and shopping trolleys is clearly a fantasy which the writer knows would never happen.
Any idea of a resemblance between the mindless violence of football hooligans and the occasional minor inconveniences and misfortunes caused by mothers wheeling perambulators, shoppers with trolleys and elderly people, all of them walking in pedestrian areas, is so far-fetched as to suggest monstrous and humorous exaggeration of the small grain of a genuine grievance being expressed.

Practice passages

First passage

As we got nearer to the larger of the Brothers we could see that it rose sheer
out of the sea, the cliffs being some two hundred feet high. On top of a flat
area at the edge of the cliffs crouched what appeared to be a baby crane
looking, as cranes always do, like a surrealistic giraffe. The launch headed for
5 the cliffs below the crane and we could see a group of three people standing
around its base; they waved vaguely at us and we waved back.

'I suppose,' I asked Brian, 'that that crane's the way they get supplies on to
the island?'

'It's the way they get everything on to the island,' said Brian.

10 'Everything?' asked Jim. 'What d'you mean by everything?'

'Well, if you want to get on to the island you've got to go by crane. There is
a path up the cliffs, but you could never land on the rocks in this sort of
weather. No, they'll lower the net down in a minute and have you up there in
a jiffy.'

15 'D'you mean to say they're thinking of hauling us up that cliff in a *net*?'
asked Jim.

'Yes,' said Brian.

Just at that moment the skipper of the launch cut the engines down, and we
drifted under the cliff, rising and falling on the blue-green swell and watching
20 the breakers cream and suck at the jagged cliff some twenty-five feet away.
The nose of the crane appeared high above, and from it dangled—at the end
of an extremely fragile-looking hawser—something closely resembling a
gigantic pig net. The crane uttered a series of clankings, groans and shrieks
that were quite audible, even above the noise of the wind and the sea, and the
25 pig net started to descend. Jim gave me a mute look of anguish and I must say
that I sympathised with him. I have no head for heights at all and I did not
relish, any more than he did, being hauled up that cliff in a pig net slung on
the end of a crane that, from the sound of it, was a very frail octogenarian
who had been without the benefit of oil for a considerable number of years.
30 Chris, wrapped up in his duffle coat and looking more like a disgruntled Duke
of Wellington than ever, started Organising with the same fanatical gleam in
his eye that Brian always had in similar situations.

'Now I want you to go up first, Jim, and get the camera set up by the crane
so that you can film Gerry and Jacquie as they land,' he said. 'I'll go up next
35 and get shots of the launch from the net, and then Gerry and Jacquie will
follow with the rest of the equipment. Okay?'

'No,' said Jim. 'Why should *I* have to go first? Supposing the thing breaks
just as I get to the top? Have you seen the rocks down here?'

'Well, if it breaks we'll know it's unsafe and go back to Picton,' said
40 Jacquie sweetly.

Jim gave her a withering look as he reluctantly climbed into the pig net,
which had by now landed on the tiny deck of the launch. The skipper waved

his hand, there was a most terrifying screech of tortured metal, and Jim,
clinging desperately to the mesh of the pig net, rose slowly and majestically
45 into the air, whirling slowly round and round.

'I wonder if he gets net-sick as well as sea-sick?' said Jacquie.

'Sure to,' said Chris callously. 'To the best of my knowledge he gets sea-
sick, train-sick, car-sick, plane-sick and home-sick, so I can't see him escaping being net-sick as well.'

50 Jim was now about half-way up, still twisting round and round, his white
face peering down at us from between the meshes of the net.

'We're all *mad*,' we heard him yell above the sound of the sea and the infernal noise the crane was making. He was still yelling presumably insulting
remarks at us when the net disappeared over the edge of the cliff.

(a) Explain how the writer gradually reveals the significance of the crane in the
first lines of the passage.

(b) Why is the crane described as 'crouching' (l. 3) rather than 'standing' on the
cliff?

(c) Why does the writer liken a crane to a surrealistic giraffe (l. 4)?

(d) What does the fact that the word 'net' in line 15 is in italics convey about
Jim's reaction to the information he has just received?

(e) Comment on the writer's use of the word 'cream' in line 20 in describing
what was happening to the breakers against the cliff.

(f) Quote the words which appear later in the passage which partly explain the
various noises referred to in line 23.

(g) What related impressions of the crane does the writer suggest in the words 'a
very frail octogenarian' (l. 28)?

(h) What impression is given of Chris by the use of the capital letter at the beginning
of Organising in line 31?

(i) Comment on the use of the word 'sweetly' in line 40 as related to Jacquie's
foregoing remark.

(j) Comment on the effect of the writer's inclusion of the word 'majestically'
among the other details of Jim's ascent.

Second passage

The train stopped just before sunrise at Ur Junction. This is merely a buffet
for locomotives which, having drunk there, go onward to the Persian Gulf.

No sooner had I stepped down on the track than I became aware of
something familiar. I had often seen the Junction before. It was the lonely
5 station of the silent films, where the hero arrives in circumstances which never
vary. First, a towering locomotive with its chain of shining Pullman coaches
would charge the spectator at full speed, swerving at the moment of impact to
draw gently to a halt. Then the hero would descend, casting glances of dismay
at a landscape in whose complete desolation the tracks converge towards the
10 horizon. As if to accentuate his abandonment, full attention was given to the

train's departure. There were pictures of the passengers, of helpful negro attendants, of wheels gathering speed, and eventually the hero would be left alone, standing in a dazed condition on the permanent way.

15 Every detail of this scene was reproduced at Ur in the half-light of that morning. There was nothing but the station and the railway lines drawn north and south. The air was piercing and cold, and the silence was intense. The very fact that I had arrived in comfort in a train now seemed to make Ur more desolate and remote than I could have imagined.

Unlike my predecessors in this situation, I was not met by a girl swinging a
20 sun-bonnet or by an ancient man driving a buggy, or even by a crowd of rusticated persons who always came to the rescue of the man in a film. There was nothing at Ur but dawn breaking over the flat land. As the light grew stronger, it served only to reveal a wider wilderness. But when the sun rose, it shone on a remarkable feature of the landscape. About two miles away a
25 mound of reddish earth rose like a pyramid with a crushed apex. It was an enormous structure, and it was unmistakably the famous Ziggurat of Ur. I had seen many a photograph of it and had read about it in many a book; and there it was in the lonely early morning, only a short walk away across the desert.

30 As I drew near to it across a dry, salty marsh, I could see in the sharp sunlight that it was not a mound of earth, neither was it shapeless: it was a great structure of mud brick, and the ramps which led to its summit were clearly defined, even from this distance.

I had not realised that the Ziggurat of Ur would be so impressive, or that so
35 much of it remained. All these temple towers of Babylonia and Chaldea were of the same design: a series of vast, almost square platforms rising one above the other, each platform smaller than the one below. Every nursery makes ziggurats with those bricks that fit one inside another! The shrine of the god was on the top-most platform, and huge inclined ramps led up to it from the ground level.

40 Impressive as the Ziggurat of Ur is, even in decay, it must have been an amazing sight when the platforms rose above the plain in bands of vivid colour, the lower stages in black, the upper in red, and the shrine in blue with a roof of gilded metal. And when the priests in coloured robes ascended and descended the ramps, or escorted the statue of the deity down to some great
45 festival, well may the scene have inspired, as Sir Leonard Woolley suggests it may have done, the dream of Jacob's Ladder, with its train of angels going up and down.

(a)   In what sense is Ur Junction a buffet for locomotives (l. 1–2)?

(b)   Why might the writer have chosen the expression 'became aware of' (l. 3) in preference to 'noticed'?

(c)   'I had often seen the Junction before' (l. 4). What does the writer really mean here?

(d)   Why does the writer refer to a *chain* of Pullman coaches (l. 6)?

(e)   Comment on the use of the word 'charge' (l. 7) to describe the movement of the filmed train.

(f)   What impression of the surroundings is given by the expression 'the tracks converge towards the horizon' (l. 9–10)?

(g)   What is the writer's purpose in referring to his recollections of silent films?

(h)   In what sense was the air 'piercing' (l. 16)?

(i)   Why would the fact that the writer arrived in comfort in a train seem 'to make Ur more desolate and remote' (l. 17–18)?

(j)   What circumstance accentuates the enormous size of the Ziggurat?

(k)   Why are the words 'ascended' and 'descended' (l. 43–44) more suitable here than the words 'went up and down'?

Third passage

Gabler returned to the Britannia in a far less buoyant frame of mind than he had left it. He wanted time to think over his discoveries of the morning. He wanted to dispel the vision of Kenneth Nicolls disappearing into a bog of in-explicable circumstances. He wanted to recharge the batteries of his bad
5   temper. Most of all, he wanted an opponent. Allies never did Everett Gabler half as much good as a target.

He received unexpected help as soon as he set foot in the lobby. The manager awaited him, with half a dozen aides-de-camp spread out in battle formation. The manager was a small man who normally comported himself
10   with a stately dignity. Now he was literally dancing with suppressed fury that struck answering sparks from Gabler before a word had been spoken.

'Aha, I have been waiting. I have to report to you an unparalleled outrage!' The manager rang up the curtain with slow, venomous articulation.

'Yes?' Gabler saved his powder.
15   'After breakfast the maid, Cassandra, comes to me in unimaginable woe!' Three thousand years of dramatic tradition brought the manager to an artful pause. Then, he picked up his tale in a quickened tempo. 'She tells me that Mr. Nicolls' room has again been broken into. She describes to me the horror, the devastation! She tells me of her shock and terror. She weeps!'
20   Gabler had no time for Cassandra's sensibilities. He was urging his numbed faculties into attack. 'Again? But this is outrageous, Mr. Tsaras!'

'It is indeed an outrage of which we speak,' Tsaras hissed. 'Who is this Mr. Nicolls? Is the Hotel Britannia then a den of thieves? Do we cater for gangsters and mobsters? Mr. Nicolls has been absent for a week, and twice,
25   brigands have broken down our doors.

Gabler met fire with ice.

'I am shocked that you can speak of a repetition of this event as if it were in any way Mr. Nicolls' fault.'

'Repetition!' Tsaras paused, then gave an affected laugh. 'Ha! It is more
30   than a repetition. This time there has been outright theft, wanton destruction. It is a progression. Who can tell what these assassins will do next! Will I arrive to find Cassandra and Iphigenia slaughtered? Lying in their gore? I an-

nounce to you that I can no longer be responsible!'

'That will scarcely alter the situation. You have already been irresponsible.'

35 Gabler did a little artful pausing himself. 'There has been grossly inadequate supervision of valuable personal property.'

Tsaras sucked in his breath. The litany of all hotel managers on such occasions rose automatically to his lips. 'Guests are requested to deposit valuables in the hotel safe.'

40 'That in no way relieves the manager of the duty to take ordinary precautions,' Gabler said sternly. He instantly followed up his advantage. 'I myself will view the scene. If necessary I shall demand a police investigation with full publicity. I may even speak to the Greek Tourist Board.'

Tsaras paled. He knew he had gone too far.

(a) Suggest the effect the writer is seeking to create in the first paragraph by the repetition of 'he wanted' as the main element in four consecutive sentences.

(b) How appropriate do you consider the association of a person's mysterious disappearance with 'a bog of inexplicable circumstances'. (lines 3–4)?

(c) Why are the people surrounding the manager referred to as 'aides-de-camp' (l. 8) rather than just as 'assistants'?

(d) What are three other words or phrases in the first half of the passage which suggest some kind of contest between the manager and Tsaras?

(e) Comment on the use of the old-fashioned expression 'comported himself' in line 9 rather than 'behaved' in the context in which it appears.

(f) What slightly surprising effect does the addition of the word 'literally' in line 10 have?

(g) Suggest a criticism of the use of the word 'suppressed' as used in line 10.

(h) Comment on the effectiveness of 'The manager rang up the curtain' (l. 13) in preference to 'The manager started speaking'.

(i) Suggest three ways in which the manager was able to achieve a dramatic effect in the way he spoke.

(j) Relate the sentence 'Gabler met fire with ice' (l. 26) to the contrasting ways in which Gabler and Tsaras express themselves.

(k) How does the writer show that Gabler could choose very effective weapons in gaining a victory over his opponent?

2 Reading comprehension

Section A: Vocabulary Choice Sentences

In this section you must choose the word or phrase which best completes each sentence. Write the number of each sentence and after it the letter A, B, C, D or E for the answer you choose. *Give one answer only* to each question.

Group 1

1 Rain and sun had swelled the pea _____ , so that the peas nestling inside were almost ready to be extracted and cooked.
   A husks   **B** shells   **C** pods   **D** cells   **E** rinds

2 He awaited the verdict of the case with _____ as so little seemed to have been achieved in proving his innocence.
   A dread   **B** timidity   **C** fright   **D** shock   **E** panic

3 Nothing would _____ me to fly except in a case of extreme emergency.
   A encourage   **B** recommend   **C** influence   **D** stimulate
   E induce

4 The _____ which led to the accident must be carefully investigated.
   A position   **B** consequences   **C** circumstances   **D** eventualities
   E cause

5 Sprawled luxuriously in front of the fire, a sleek tabby cat was contentedly _____.
   A chuckling   **B** purring   **C** growling   **D** humming
   E snoring

6 WANTED: A sensible and _____ person to assist with kitchen and cleaning duties.
   A talented   **B** serious   **C** worthy   **D** skilful   **E** capable

7 He has _____ the management with negligence in having failed to provide protection against possible dangerous fume leakage.
   A challenged   **B** attacked   **C** defied   **D** charged   **E** accused

8 It is hoped that some solution of the _____ between the management and the union will be found at today's meeting.
   A discussion   **B** dispute   **C** argument   **D** debate
   E controversy

94

9   Most cheaper furniture is made of a utility wood and then covered with a
    thin _____ of wood of a higher quality.
    A varnish   **B** surface   **C** coating   **D** veneer   **E** casing

10 Your pronunciation would improve if you _____ with a tape recorder.
    A exercised   **B** repeated   **C** practised   **D** trained   **E** drilled

Group 2

1   The strikers have _____ yesterday's pay offer from the employers.
    A denied   **B** disagreed with   **C** withdrawn   **D** rejected
    E turned away

2   This is the third episode in the _____ series of programmes based on the
    travels of Marco Polo.
    A actual   **B** present-day   **C** current   **D** topical   **E** existing

3   First he tapped with a pencil and then with his fingers until his constant
    _____ began to get on my nerves.
    A fidgeting   **B** wriggling   **C** twitching   **D** flickering
    E quivering

4   Leaving a car in a no-parking area is one of the commonest traffic
    _____.
    A offences   **B** problems   **C** crimes   **D** faults
    E commitments

5   Believing herself alone in the house she was _____ when she heard
    someone unknown moving about in the hall.
    A incredulous   **B** stunned   **C** startled   **D** aghast
    E annoyed

6   You will have to _____ this report for the Committee as there are several
    possible misstatements in it.
    A restore   **B** renew   **C** repair   **D** revise   **E** reform

7   You can't change what you did in the past so stop _____ and looking
    miserable and come and enjoy yourself.
    A meditating   **B** considering   **C** reflecting   **D** brooding
    E speculating

8   Your passport is out of date and you have no permit to work here: we must
    _____ ask you to leave the country within three days.
    A thus   **B** in effect   **C** nevertheless   **D** even so
    E accordingly

9   He _____ along so vigorously that his companion had to run to keep up
    with him.
    A tramped   **B** strode   **C** strutted   **D** strolled   **E** shuffled

10 The firm will not _____ give you a pension when you retire: this will de-
    pend on your length of service.
    A necessarily   **B** certainly   **C** surely   **D** naturally   **E** consequently

Group 3

1 He intends to _____ the secretary he has dismissed by a less glamorous but rather more efficient one.
A replace B substitute C make way for D allow for
E supersede

2 At last they had invented an aeroplane that could break _____ the sound barrier.
A up B out of C down D through E into

3 After three days without food he _____ towards the farmhouse and collapsed on the doorstep.
A waddled B stammered C wobbled D swayed
E staggered

4 Please _____ my greetings to all our mutual friends.
A carry B convey C transmit D transport E transfer

5 'Really, I can't think anybody could be interested in that,' he _____ in an affected tone, as if he were too bored to speak at all.
A muttered B whispered C drawled D mumbled
E lisped

6 The standard of his work is _____ : at times extremely good but at others mediocre or even worthless.
A varied B contrasting C variable D different E various

7 His doctor _____ him to take time off to recover fully but he said there was nobody to replace him at work.
A convinced B persuaded C suggested D incited
E advised

8 A green carpet of _____ covered the decaying tree trunk.
A turf B shrub C mushroom D moss E herb

9 He is trying to _____ for at least some of the suffering he has caused.
A repay B reward C recompense D remunerate
E make amends

10 My landlord has recently signed an agreement renewing my _____ of his flat for a further two years.
A tenancy B occupation C residence D possession
E ownership

Group 4

1 Dark glasses serve to _____ the eyes from the glare of the sun.
A shroud B save C shelter D shield E defend

2 You know that smoking always brings _____ a fit of coughing.
A on B in C up D to E out

96

3 The springlike weather_____ me to go out for a walk but I knew that if I did, I should not finish the letter in time.
   A attracted **B** coaxed **C** tempted **D** compelled **E** lured

4 Immense areas of fertile soil have been lost as a result of_____.
   A demolition **B** decay **C** ruin **D** destruction **E** erosion

5 Anyone who drives under the influence of drink is_____ of any responsibility for other people's safety.
   A negligent **B** careless **C** reckless **D** carefree **E** heedless

6 We know that Smith was involved in the burglary and we believe that Jones and Robinson were his_____ .
   A partners **B** colleagues **C** accomplices **D** fellows
   E collaborators

7 He was _____ at the police station for several hours for intensive questioning.
   A delayed **B** deterred **C** kept back **D** retained
   E detained

8 He showed only_____ enthusiasm when I suggested a skiing holiday and appeared to have other ideas of his own.
   A mediocre **B** medium **C** average **D** moderate
   E normal

9 I don't just dislike the horrible smell from this factory: I absolutely _____it.
   A despise **B** scorn **C** object to **D** have an aversion to
   E loathe

10 Throughout centuries of burning heat, the old walls had gradually _____and little was left of them now.
   A crumbled **B** shattered **C** crunched **D** crumpled
   E powdered

Section B: Passages for Comprehension

In this section you will find after each of the passages a number of questions or unfinished statements about the passage, each with four suggested answers or ways of finishing it. You must choose the one which you think fits best. Write the number of each question and after it the letter A, B, C or D for the answer you choose. *Give one answer only* to each question.
Read each passage right through before choosing your answers.

First passage

Having finished his breakfast in peace, Harry Buckle set out on a leisurely tour of the grounds. With the house itself he was already familiar, for Thomas

had seen to that: indeed, there was something wonderful in the way that he, longing to discard it, had exposed its every defect and blemish. The various
5 stairs that were taller or shorter than the rest, so that running down you could easily trip and break your neck: the windows that could not be opened, for fear of their tumbling out altogether: floorboards unsafe as thawing ice: the likelihood that before very long part of the roof would fall in; and the certainty that if fire broke out the whole place would burn to the ground before
10 help could arrive, and yourself with it if you happened to be in one of the towers—all these matters, and the impossibility of ever finding people to set them right, had been scrupulously brought to the young man's attention.

And the house had seemed to respond to the generosity of its owner, discovering a range of resource new even to him. He was well used to a stream
15 of various small insects emerging when he turned on a bathtap, but to these were now added twigs, leaves and feathers, which he identified as from the rookery, although he was quite at a loss to determine how they entered the system. The family portraits began falling to earth like so many ripe plums. More spectacular still, the water tank overflowed: walking up the drive, the
20 two young men found an inexplicable wave rushing down it towards them, and ever since then the plumbing had moaned and gurgled like a fiend in torment.

'Who knows what it may think of next?' said Thomas, to whom the place was a living being, sentient and malign. 'There's nothing I'd put beyond it.'
25 But these and other capers only attached Mr. Buckle the more.

For the lands, however, he had feelings of another sort. He was going to bring them back into kindness. He would restore the shrubberies, rid the orchards of disease, revive the fruit and vegetable gardens, return the lawns to their ancient beauty, clear and stock the streams, plant flowers everywhere.
30 There should be lambs, chickens, calves, piglets, wandering freely in sun or rain under the sky, not gasping out their lives in cells and catacombs. It was something of a programme, perhaps, but he was quite resolved to carry it through.

He wandered out to the terrace and stood awhile, drinking the prospect in.
35 The weather held, the sun poured down, the sea twinkled and shimmered, in the sky there was hardly a cloud. It would of course not be always so. There were gales to come, and stinging rain, angry white-crested waves, falling trees, floods; but for the moment it seemed like heaven itself. At the sight of his maltreated car, he chuckled aloud. The to-do in London if somebody's paint
40 got a scratch! Here, nothing of the sort mattered at all. He felt blissfully reborn into another world of broader and kinder dimensions, infinitely rich and promising all the heart could desire.

1 The way in which Thomas showed Harry the house is referred to as 'something wonderful' because

A he had been willing to give so much time and trouble to the task

B his desire to show only its imperfections was truly amazing

C no one with any sense would have done it in this way

D despite his eagerness to dispose of it, he had made no attempt to conceal its drawbacks

2   Why were the stairs dangerous?

A Some of the staircases were higher than others

B The stairs themselves were of differing widths

C The stairs varied in height

D The flights of stairs varied in steepness

3   Some of the floorboards were unsafe because

A one might easily fall through them

B they were so highly polished that they were very slippery

C dampness spreading over the surface made them treacherous

D they were liable to collapse when the weather was particularly cold

4   Another drawback that Harry Buckle had been informed about was that

A he would inevitably be burnt alive in case of fire

B it was impossible to find anyone to run the place

C there was no hope of getting anything done about the defects

D there was a considerable danger of an outbreak of fire

5   What were the owner's reactions to the appearance of twigs, leaves and feathers?

A He had no idea about how they had got there

B He had long been accustomed to them

C He could not think where they had come from

D Apart from recognising their nature he knew nothing further about them

6   What was Harry Buckle's attitude towards these various discomforts?

A He felt that the house was hostile to him

B He feared he would never be able to escape from the house

C He sensed that the situation was deteriorating all the time

D He became increasingly fond of the house

7   One of Harry Buckle's plans for the grounds was to

A give freedom to the animals that had been shut up there

B create new and beautiful lawns

C provide ideal conditions for the wild life

D improve the condition of the fruit trees

8   What were his feelings as he stood on the terrace?

A He brooded over how desolate everything would be in bad weather

B He was thrilled by the magnificence of the angry sea

C He felt intense pleasure in his surroundings

D He realised that the beauty of the surroundings would make up for the defects in the house

9　What were Harry Buckle's reactions when he noticed his car?

   A　There was far less risk of damaging his car here than in London

   B　There would be nobody here to carry out repairs and renovations to the car

   C　He would no longer have to worry about the appearance of his car

   D　The kind-hearted people who lived here would help him to put his car to rights

Second passage

He was not only bewildered, he was completely at sea. He knew almost nothing about what surrounded him. The house he had glimpsed on arrival was certainly a substantial mansion of respectable antiquity, and he had so far been in no more then a kind of independent wing or annex added at a later
5　date. The girl calling herself Diana Mariner had said something implying that, when not actually let, the main house remained untenanted—this since her father, even when at home, was restricted to a simple way of life. But Honeybath could now believe no word that he had been told by these people. If he managed to penetrate to the main house (where his instinct for explora-
10　tion lay), there was no valid reason for believing that it would in fact prove to be deserted. The Mariners themselves might have retreated to it, for all he knew.

He switched on his torch, and crept downstairs. There was an element of irrationality in this, since the light was almost as likely to betray him as was
15　any slight noise he might make. He had no choice in the matter, however, since it would be impossible to move at all in mere darkness. But he arrived without misadventure in a small square hall which he remembered pretty well. In one wall there was only the outer door by which he had arrived, flanked by a window on either hand. The walls on either side each showed a couple of
20　doors. On the fourth side there was only one door, centrally placed, and it was distinguished from all the others by being covered in green baize. It might well lead to kitchens and the like, but he took a guess that it in fact represented a means of communication with the main dwelling. He pulled it cautiously open, and found that it then remained in this position of its own
25　accord. But what his torch now revealed behind the door was a perfectly smooth wall. He put his free hand on this and moved it over the surface. The result was a strong impression that what confronted him was a sheet of steel.

Just what he thought of this was not clear to Honeybath, but his immediate action was to move to one of the windows; he slipped behind a curtain and
30　peered out. Or, to be more exact, he thought to peer out, but was stopped by the disconcerting realisation that between himself and the external world there was something less vulnerable than a mere pane of glass. There was a fine steel shutter as well. He was in a prison. Or if he wasn't in a prison he was in a fortress. There seemed to be no means of telling which.
35　He let the torch play round the hall again. It was furnished with a

restrained elegance wholly inappropriate in the light of this grim discovery. On the floor lay a couple of Persian rugs which would certainly realise in a saleroom enough to stock several large cellars with the kind of claret offered to him at dinner. The few pieces of furniture had begun life in France
40 some centuries ago. On delicate pedestals round the walls stood small bronze figures which at once spoke to his trained sense of the Italy of the *cinque-cento*. The place was certainly no thieves' kitchen. Honeybath was astonished that he hadn't become aware of its respectable opulence before. He wondered momentarily whether one of those falling bricks hadn't hit him on the head.
45 He must certainly have been in a fairly witless condition earlier that night.

And this thought had an almost immediate physical effect. He had gone back to the door that wasn't a door, and was playing the torch again on its blank surface, when a momentary giddiness overtook him. He put out a hand to steady himself, and became aware to his horror that he had grasped one of
50 the delicate bronze figures. It moved and was almost certainly going to fall with a crash to the floor. Only it didn't fall; it simply twisted oddly in his grasp. And at once the smooth sheet of white-painted steel moved silently sideways and vanished.

There was a dark corridor in front of him.

1   What did the writer know about his surroundings?

   A   He knew only that he was in a large old house
   B   He knew he was somewhere on the coast
   C   He was very vague about what part of the country he was in
   D   He knew a little about the building he was in

2   What did he know about the girl?

   A   Her name
   B   That Diana Mariner was not her real name
   C   The name he had been given by her
   D   The name she was called by

3   What information had he got about her father?

   A   He preferred to live quietly
   B   It was necessary for him to live economically
   C   He was accustomed to a simple way of life
   D   He did his best not to attract attention by the way he lived

4   What possibility did the writer bear in mind when considering exploring the main house?

   A   There would not be anybody living there
   B   The girl and her father might be living there
   C   The house might be quite empty
   D   There would certainly be somebody living there

5 How did he feel about switching on his torch?

    A It would give away the fact that he was there
    B It was a senseless action
    C It was an unavoidable risk
    D It was an unreasonable thing to do

6 Why was he forced to use the torch?

    A He could not find his way without it
    B He would probably make less noise
    C He wanted to find a way to escape
    D He wanted to explore his surroundings

7 The steel window-covering made him wonder

    A whether this was designed for protection
    B whether it was there to stop him escaping
    C if it was there to keep people out
    D just what its purpose was

8 The elegance of the furnishings was somewhat unexpected because

    A he could not understand why so much luxury should exist in an unoccupied house
    B it seemed out of place in such a securely guarded room
    C its selling-price could have amply provided for its owner's more expensive tastes
    D he could not understand why he was being held captive in such luxurious surroundings

9 The writer considered that something might be wrong with his mind because

    A such a high standard of luxury must be some kind of delusion
    B it had taken so long for him to notice the luxury
    C his earlier impressions had so much misled him
    D he had actually assumed that the place belonged to criminals

10 Where was the bronze figure that he touched?

    A Fixed to the wall
    B Attached to the fourth door
    C Attached to the steel door
    D Standing on something

Third passage

    I remember one splendid morning, all blue and silver, in the summer holidays, when I reluctantly tore myself away from the task of doing nothing in particular, and put on a hat of some sort and picked up a walking-stick, and put six very brightly-coloured chalks in my pocket. I then went into the kitchen
5 (which, along with the rest of the house, belonged to a very square and sensi-

ble old woman in a Sussex village), and asked the owner and occupant of the kitchen if she had any brown paper. She had a great deal; in fact, she had too much; and she mistook the reason and the justification for the existence of brown paper. She seemed to have an idea that if a person wanted brown

10 paper he must be wanting to tie up parcels, which was the last thing I wanted to do; indeed, it is a thing which I have found to be beyond my mental capacity. Hence she dwelt very much on the varying qualities of toughness and endurance in the material. I explained to her that I only wanted to draw pictures on it, and that I did not want them to endure in the least; and that from my

15 point of view, therefore, it was a question not of tough consistency, but of responsive surface, a thing comparatively irrelevant in a parcel. When she understood that I wanted to draw she offered to overwhelm me with notepaper, apparently supposing that I did my notes and correspondence on old brown paper wrappers from motives of economy.

20 I then tried to explain the rather delicate logical shade, that I not only liked brown paper, but liked the quality of brownness in paper, just as I liked the quality of brownness in October woods, or in beer, or in the peat-streams of the North. Brown paper represents the primal twilight of the first toil of creation, and with a bright-coloured chalk or two you can pick out points of fire in

25 it, sparks of gold, and blood-red, and sea-green, like the first fierce stars that sprang out of divine darkness. All this I said (in an off-hand way) to the old woman; and I put the brown paper in my pocket along with the chalks, and possibly other things.

With my stick and my knife, my chalks and my brown paper, I went out on

30 to the great downs. I wandered over the rolling countryside, crossed one swell of living turf after another, looking for a place to sit down and draw. Do not, for heaven's sake, imagine I was going to sketch from Nature. I was going to draw devils and seraphim, and blind old gods that men worshipped before the dawn of right, and saints in robes of angry crimson, and seas of strange green,

35 and all the sacred or monstrous symbols that look so well in bright colours on brown paper. They are much better worth drawing than Nature; also they are much easier to draw. When a cow came slouching by in the field next to me, a mere artist might have drawn it; but I always get wrong in the hind legs of quadrupeds. So I drew the soul of the cow; which I saw there plainly walking

40 before me in the sunlight; and the soul was all purple and silver, and had seven horns and the mystery that belongs to all the beasts. But though I could not with a crayon get the best out of the landscape, it does not follow that the landscape was not getting the best out of me.

1 What was the writer's attitude towards his intended outing?

A He did not want to go
B There was no other way of passing the time
C He had to make an effort to get started
D He decided to go because he did not enjoy having too little to do

2   What was the woman's reaction to the writer's request?

   A   She could not understand what he said
   B   She could not imagine what he could want brown paper for
   C   She wanted to know why he wanted brown paper
   D   She showed that she had the wrong idea about what brown paper is really for

3   What were the writer's feelings about tying up parcels?

   A   He might have done this if he had been cleverer
   B   He would use the paper for this only after he had done all the other things he wanted to do with it
   C   He found the idea of doing this extraordinary
   D   He was not interested in the idea of tying up parcels

4   He wanted paper that

   A   was not too stiff to use for drawing
   B   had lightness and flexibility
   C   was very strong and would last a long time
   D   would be an effective material for drawing on

5   The quality required for drawing paper

   A   would be of little importance in paper used for parcels
   B   would make it useless for wrapping parcels
   C   was seldom found in wrapping paper
   D   was totally unnecessary in wrapping paper

6   The woman wanted to give him notepaper because she probably

   A   thought he considered using notepaper something of an extravagance
   B   imagined he had run out of notepaper
   C   thought the idea of writing letters on brown paper was an extraordinary one
   D   suspected he wanted to keep the brown paper he had for writing letters

7   Why did the writer like brown paper for drawing?

   A   It offers an effective contrast to bright colours
   B   It combines in itself all the colours of nature
   C   The particular shade that characterises such paper appealed to him
   D   Brown is the earliest of all colours from which all others derive

8   What impression is given of the route taken by the writer across the downs?

   A   He climbed up to a place offering a good view
   B   He walked over a series of rising and descending slopes
   C   He moved from one area of grassland to another
   D   He crossed a succession of small streams

9   What did the artist draw on his brown paper?

   A   An abstract painting unrelated to his surroundings
   B   Primitive natural forces and objects of worship

    C   Patterns and designs based on ancient symbols

    D   His own interpretation of what he saw

10   What did the subjects of the writer's drawings have in common?

    A   They had all existed for a very long time

    B   None of them had ever existed as human beings

    C   They were all objects of heathen worship

    D   They all fired the writer's imagination

3 Use of English

Section A: Structural and Grammatical Exercises

1 Fill each of the numbered blanks in the following passages with *one* suitable word.

1 (*a*) Most people usually manage to remain on reasonably good _____ (1) with their neighbours. This is _____ (2) easier in many cases by the _____ (3) that couples at work during the day and often _____ (4) relatives at week-ends may have little contact with their neighbours. However, disagreements and even bitter quarrels are by no _____ (5) uncommon. Neighbours' pets, in _____ (6) their cats, recognise no boundaries to private property, and their intrusion may be resented by a neighbour who does not _____ (7) their owners' affection for them and regards his broken plants _____ (8) justifiable _____ (9). Children _____ (10) lost balls in neighbours' gardens _____ (11) permission and helping _____ (12) to apples and flowers on the way, frequent noisy parties continuing into the small _____ (13), sarcastic remarks about next door's plaster rabbits overheard from the nearby lawn, _____ (14) from smouldering bonfires blackening the freshly-laundered _____ (15): all these irritations can result _____ (16) angry words and even references to solicitors and law-suits. However, harmony is more common than discord. The garden fence serves _____ (17) a meeting-place for housewives _____ (18) food prices and the previous evening's T.V. while husbands compare car performances and weed-killers. Yet the attitude of a good-natured friend of mine is still surprisingly common. 'The people at number 49 are a thorough _____ (19). Screaming kids, a yapping dog and an eternally blaring transistor! But we're lucky in those at 45. Such nice people! In fact, we _____ (20) ever see or hear them.'

1 (*b*) While an ability to pick up languages must to a certain _____ (1) be _____ (2) to a person's general intelligence level, so many other factors are involved _____ (3) the process of language learning _____ (4) intelligence may apparently have comparatively _____ (5) influence _____ (6) actual performance. Psychological factors are probably _____ (7) the most important of these. Self-confident extroverts, who

have no hesitation _____ (8) expressing _____ (9), however _____ (10) mistakes they may_____ (11), are obviously _____ (12) an advantage. Memory plays a large_____ (13) in learning, both consciously in retaining new vocabulary and also unconsciously in storing _____ (14) many expressions heard but not_____ (15) much attention to at the time. Motivation is a major _____ (16). In order to survive in a foreign country where his own language is unknown, the newcomer is_____ (17) to pick up at_____ (18) a few essential words and constructions to cover his everyday_____ (19). It is probable,_____ (20), that even here intelligence is of service in making twenty words do the work of two hundred more or less successfully.

2 **Finish each of the following sentences in such a way that it means exactly the same as the sentence printed before it.**
Example: There must be few people so ignorant of the past as he is.
There must be few people who know . . . .
Answer: There must be few people who know so little about the past as he does.

2 (*a*) 1 Hardly anybody failed to attend the meeting.
The meeting . . . .

2 He had never before addressed such a large crowd.
The crowd . . . .

3 I shall consider this matter seriously.
I shall give . . . .

4 Few people would agree with you.
There aren't . . . .

5 He threatened to resign if they did not give him a rise.
He warned . . . .

6 It was only after I had read the last sentence that I realised how important the letter was.
Not until . . . .

7 'If you hear anyone trying to get in,' he said to me, 'telephone the police.'
He told . . . .

8 I wrote the announcement in large black letters because I wanted everybody to notice it.
I wrote the announcement in large black letters so . . . .

9 Your arguments have had very little influence on him.
He is far from . . . .

10 There were four people in the doctor's waiting-room, including myself.
I was one . . . .

2 (b) 1 He did not start speaking until the whole class was attending to him.
He waited until . . . .

2 I followed the doctor's orders exactly.
I did . . . .

3 'You must spend a week on the island next spring, but don't go there
before May,' she told me.
She recommended . . . .

4 She had two candles ready on the table as there might be a power cut.
She had two candles ready on the table, lest . . . .

5 His rapid recovery was due to skilled medical attention.
As a result . . . .

6 This door may be used only in an emergency.
Only . . . .

7 He has been speaking for three hours.
It is . . . .

8 My anxiety was quite unnecessary.
I . . . .

9 'Why did you choose to study Latin?' he asked me.
He asked me the . . . .

10 He had complete confidence in his ability to deal with the matter.
He was quite sure that . . . .

2 (c) 1 'If Roberts offers you any money, don't accept it,' he said to me.
He advised me not . . . .

2 He completed the novel only after five years.
It took him . . . .

3 The explorers meant to follow the river to its source.
The explorers' . . . .

4 The foundation stone was laid in 1950, but it was not until twenty years
later that this great cathedral was completed.
It took twenty years . . . .

5 My cat and my dog are on very friendly terms.
My cat and my dog get . . . .

6 Watching football on television rarely interests my wife.
My wife shows . . . .

7 They chattered and giggled throughout his lecture.
They chattered and giggled all the . . . .

8 Her hair is exactly the same colour as her mother's is.
There is no . . . .

9 It looked like rain.
It looked as . . . .

108

10 It's getting very late. We ought to go home.
It's high time we . . . .

3 Fill each of the numbered blanks with *one* suitable word or phrase.
Example: Erica has been out of work for two months. I do hope she soon
succeeds . . . .
Answer: in finding a job, in finding something to do.

3 (a) 1 He was delighted when, at his fourth attempt, he at last succeeded
. . . . .his final examination.

2 She has been playing the piano continuously and very badly for three
hours. I do wish . . . .

3 I could have looked up the meaning of those new words if I
. . . .

4 My briefcase must be somewhere or other but I've no idea
. . . . .be.

5 Andrew: 'What's wrong with the electric bell today?'
Ann: 'I don't know. It just . . . .'

6 There is a tiny crack in one of my teeth. I'll have to go to the dentist and
. . . .

7 When I heard the crash in the street outside, I went to the window to
see what . . . .

8 I can hear angry voices from the boys' room. They seem
. . . .

3 (b) 1 'I'm so sorry I couldn't get here any sooner. You do look rather cold. I
hope you . . . . .long.'

2 Peter (telephoning): 'I had to spend all night in my car in a snowdrift.'
Paul: 'My goodness! How cold you . . . .'

3 You eat too much. You would lose weight if you . . . .'

4 What a pity one has to spend so much time working! There are so
many interesting things to do if only one . . . .

5 Those small boats sailing into the harbour would make a wonderful
photograph, but I've got nothing to take one with. I wish
. . . . .with me.

6 Unfortunately it isn't always true that the harder you work,
. . . . .Not in my job, anyway.

7 I hardly recognised your daughter when we met. After all, it was ten
years since I . . . .

8 They couldn't persuade him to fly to France as he hated flying, but he
wasn't opposed to . . . . .sea.

3 (c) 1 He won't listen to anything you say. It's no use . . . .

2 When he caught sight of the elephant, the child stopped, open-mouthed, and I realised that this was probably the first time he . . . .

3 She put the fragile glass vase on the table extremely carefully so as . . . . .it.

4 He had been completely silent in the meeting until they started discussing the new wage rates and only then . . . . .opinion.

5 I refuse to accept such untidy and careless work. It must . . . .

6 Tom: 'But it's a two-hour walk from here. Won't your wife get very tired?'
Tim:'Not a bit. She used to walk ten kilometres every day and often farther. She is used . . . .

7 He . . . . .tested last week and was told he would need stronger glasses.

8 I really don't know about this picture but it just . . . . .painted by Goya.

9 I have come across some superb tapestries on my travels but that one on your wall is the most beautiful that I . . . .

4 **For each of the sentences below, write a new sentence *as similar as possible in meaning to the original sentence*, but using the word given in capital letters.**
   Example: The fortune-teller's warning impressed the emperor far more than anyone would have expected.
   IMPRESSION
   Answer: The fortune-teller's warning made a far greater impression on the emperor than anyone would have expected.

4 (a) 1 We discussed the new project in detail.
   DISCUSSION

2 Some problems are inevitable if you go to live in another country.
   BOUND

3 Whether he is worshipped or despised is all the same to him.
   DIFFERENCE

4 The police have told Bert that they believe it was he who stole the car.
   CHARGED

5 At last I slipped a five-pound note into his hand and it was only then that he gave me the information.
   UNTIL

6 He has had to give up his legal practice because he is so often ill.
   REASON

7 Try not to make any more noise than you can help.
POSSIBLE

8 Speaking personally, I could stay here for ever.
CONCERNED

9 For a moment she thought he was her long-lost husband.
MISTOOK

10 I don't see why we must start so early.
POINT

4 (b) 1 Washing in cold water is nothing unusual for him.
USED

2 He told me that delivery of the goods before Thursday would be quite impossible for him.
UNABLE

3 He asked me if I thought it would be a good thing to buy the second-hand car.
WORTH

4 The bell in the corridor should be rung if there is a fire.
CASE

5 He next said that there were, of course, exceptions.
WENT

6 He was the only person I could trust.
THERE

7 That's not your business.
NOTHING

8 He told me he was sorry he had lost his temper.
APOLOGISED

9 He lost his job because he was often absent.
RESULT

10 Returning the same day would be senseless.
SENSE

Section B: Passages for Comprehension

Read the following passages and then answer the questions which follow them.

First passage

'Anyone who is going to look after old people ought to spend a week in an armchair, with one leg in a splint, one arm in a sling, and both ears filled with cotton wool! Then they would begin to understand what it is like to be completely helpless and dependent!'

5   That is the view of one woman who has given a good many years to this work. She feels that, despite the fact that we all know we ourselves will be old one day and at the mercy of others' good will, it is almost impossible for an active, healthy person to realise what this means. Many of the disabilities of old age and the so-called 'tiresomeness' of old people are, she suggests, the
10 fault of those who look after them.

    One example is the way they are so often presumed not to know what they want. 'May I have the window open, please?' provokes a series of objections—'Oh won't you be cold? Then hadn't you better have an extra rug or shawl?'

15   As one old lady privately observed to a visitor, 'One gives up in time. I am now too old to fight for what I want. I have learned to endure.' And yet she was surrounded by relatives who loved her and would have been horrified to realise that their anxious care was making her life a misery.

    It is curious, too, how often sympathy for the old and infirm takes a form
20 which actually humiliates them. Their friends, or mere acquaintances, wishing to show good will, paw them, sometimes leaning forward to rearrange their neckwear, pulling at their shawl, touching their hair or patting their faces—things they would never presume to do, unasked, to one of their contemporaries.

25   An equally humiliating habit of many people who are quite unconscious of being rude is to talk about old people in front of them, as if they were not there, discussing their health, or making playful remarks on the lines of 'Well, nurse, has she been a good girl today?'

    It is now universally accepted that children should be encouraged to do as
30 much as they can for themselves in order to develop their brains and muscles, but so few people today seem to have time to allow the elderly the same means of keeping their minds and muscles active. With what they believe to be unselfish kindness they perform innumerable services for them that they would be much better left to do, even with a struggle, for themselves.

35   Convenient flats, well-run homes, 'motherly' visitors, or organised entertainments cannot make up for the fundamental need which must be satisfied—the need to retain to the end of life human dignity and the respect of one's fellows.

1   What difficulties faced by many old people are mentioned in the first sentence? . . . .

2   What reason does the writer give for the insensitive way in which many well-meaning people treat the old? . . . .

3   The expression 'a good many' in line 5 could be replaced by the words . . . .

4   The words 'one day' in line 7 could be otherwise expressed as . . . .

5 The word 'this' in line 8 means..............
6 In what way is the 'tiresomeness' of old people (line 9) the fault of those who look after them?
7 'they' in line 11 refers to..............
8 The word 'series' in 'a series of objections' (line 12) suggests that there are ....
9 The words 'gives up' in line 15 can be expressed in different words as ....
10 Explain the contrast between the ideas expressed in the two halves of the fourth paragraph..............
11 What do the words 'anxious care' (line 18) suggest about the behaviour of relatives towards the old lady?..............
12 When we 'presume' to do things (line 23), we..............
13 'It is now universally accepted' (line 29) can be expressed more briefly as ....
14 Explain in what way the intelligent care of the young and the old should be similar...............
15 Summarise in about 100 words the ways in which care and attention given to old people may lower their dignity as human beings...............

Second passage

Southern England does not, for the most part, contain the wild, wide, unspoilt landscapes to be found in other parts of Britain. There are no Highlands, no Pennines, no Snowdonia, and it is only on the fringes of the West Country, in Dorset and Wiltshire, that the scale of the countryside begins to climb beyond
5 the cosy and the charming.

It is the most densely populated region of Britain, and it shows. Villages do not huddle in sheltered valleys or at moorland crossroads; they sprawl across former fields and down once-deserted lanes, forever expanding to meet the needs of prosperous newcomers.
10 In the stockbroker belt of Surrey and Kent, the planners' efforts have failed to prevent the growth of what might be described as megalocomy. This is the rural equivalent of megalopolis, a fusion of town and village which, while it may not have obliterated the countryside, has intruded upon it to the point where it is difficult to distinguish one from the other.
15 Thus Southern England has become identified with the soft life, its gentle landscape reflecting the affluent lifestyle of its inhabitants. Northerners, Scotsmen and Welshmen despise it, arguing that their wilder, less well-groomed surroundings breed a strength of character and a resolution that is lacking in the effete southerners.
20 Outdoor activities to a large extent reflect this picture. There are dozens of immaculately groomed golf courses, with annual subscriptions to match, but even the best of them do not really rate with the championship links of

Scotland and the North-west. Cricket is played on countless picturesque
village greens, but seldom with the same intensity as in Yorkshire and
25 Lancashire.

Despite occasional surprising triumphs, like Southampton winning the F.A.
Cup last season, the general standard of football and rugby is well below the
best. The prevailing image remains a Betjemanesque[1] one of tennis on the
vicarage lawn.

1   What geographical difference between Southern England and other parts of
     Britain mentioned in the first paragraph could be seen from the air?
     . . . .
2   'it' in the expressions 'it shows' in line 6 refers to . . . .
3   Explain the contrast between the villages that huddle and the villages that
     sprawl, in the second paragraph . . . .
4   How would the 'former fields' (line 8) and 'once deserted lanes' (line 8)
     appear today? . . . .
5   The   prosperous   newcomers   referred   to   in   line   9   are   people
     . . . .
6   What people mentioned in the third paragraph apparently dislike the way the
     countryside has changed? . . . .
7   Explain the suitability of the word 'intruded' in line 13 . . . .
8   What is the difference between the following:
        'it may not have obliterated the countryside' (line 13)
        'it has intruded upon it to the point where it is difficult to distinguish one
        from the other' (lines 13–14)
9   In lines 15 to 16 the 'gentle landscape' of Southern England is said to
     reflect 'the affluent lifestyle of its inhabitants'. Explain the connection
     between these two ideas. . . . .
10 Why do Northerners, Scotsmen and Welshmen despise the lifestyle of the
     residents of the stockbroker belt? . . . .
11 Suggest why the singular form of the verb 'is' follows the apparently plural sub-
     ject: 'a strength of character and a resolution' (line 18) . . . .
12 'this picture' (line 20) refers to . . . .
13 What is the usual meaning of 'groom', and how does the idea apply to its use
     in line 18 and also in line 21? . . . .
14 What contrast is suggested between sports activities in Northern and in
     Southern Britain? . . . .
15 What impression of the quality of sport in the South is given by the reference
     in line 28 to tennis? . . . .
16 Explain in about 100 words the main contrasts expressed here between the
     North and the South of Britain. . . . .

[1] John Betjeman, poet and radio and T.V. personality, is particularly associated with the quiet countryside and villages of Southern England.

114

Third passage

The second part of an investigation is interrogation or, more simply, the questioning of everyone who can throw light on the inquiry. Again, the object of the detective is to establish as far as possible an unprejudiced account of facts. In Britain, he is guided by the Judges' Rules on evidence and
5 throughout his investigation he has to keep in mind that eventually every fact, every witness he produces, will be submitted to skilled cross-examination in Court. Hearsay evidence, for example, might give him a line on the person he is seeking, but he will not be able to use it as proof of his case. He may not use force or the threat of force; nor may he use any artificial means such as
10 'truth' drugs or alcohol to get a statement from a witness or suspected person. Interviewing people within the limits prescribed by the law is extremely difficult, and a major measure of a detective's skill is his ability as an interrogator.

Questioning in an investigation ranges from the straightforward door-to-
15 door inquiry of, say, all the inhabitants of a particular street in order to establish whether they have seen a specific individual or not, to the complicated interrogation of the major culprit in a case of large-scale fraud. In the one case, the detective simply knocks at the door, announces that he is a police officer and asks a direct question: 'Did you see a tall thin man with red hair in
20 this road between six and ten o'clock last night?' The householder would have no reason for lying, and nine times out of ten the answer would be an equally direct 'Yes' or 'No'. In the other case the detective would need all his skill both to unravel the complications of the case and to know what questions to ask and how to ask them. He would try to lead the culprit gently through the
25 history of the crime in an attempt either to ease a confession out of him or to get enough information to show where further inquiries might be usefully made.

In such cases a direct question nearly always produces a direct lie, and the detective needs to be as circumspect as possible if he is to succeed in getting
30 the information he wants.

The general technique of questioning a difficult witness or suspect is to talk round the subject rather than directly about it. The detective should never appear hurried, and he should always be prepared to continue an interview for hours on end if necessary. The analogy with fishing is trite, but the detec-
35 tive is indeed very like the angler: he must wait patiently until his bait is taken and he must be careful not to strike too soon or else he will lose his fish altogether. Some people, for instance, refuse to talk at all, and they are often the most difficult to question. With them, the detective's best method is to show a great interest in the individual, to let him know how much time is
40 being spent over him, to exaggerate the importance of any slight statement he might then be induced to make, and so gently to flatter him into talking. Others cannot be stopped from talking, and with them the detective simply sits back and picks up the items he wants from the stream of words. John

George Haigh of the 'acid bath' murders, for instance, spoke for more than
45 forty hours—with intervals only for food and short rests—when he was first
invited by the C.I.D. to make a statement.

1   A person who can 'throw any light on an enquiry' (line 2) is one who
    . . . .
2   An 'unprejudiced' account of facts (line 3) is an account . . . .
3   Evidence that gives a detective 'a line on the person he is seeking' (lines 7–8) is
    useful because . . . .
4   According to the first paragraph, why is 'interviewing people within the limits
    prescribed by the law' so difficult? . . . .
5   'A major measure of a detective's skill' (line 12) can be otherwise expressed
    as . . . .
6   What information about the types of questioning is given by the use of the
    word 'ranges' in line 14?
7   A door-to-door inquiry is described as 'straightforward' (line 14) because
    . . . .
8   Two possible meanings of the word 'case' in line 17 are . . . .
9   Why would the householder in line 21 have no reason for lying?
    . . . .
10 The words 'In the other case' in line 22 refer to . . . .
11 What is usually 'unravelled' (line 23) in the literal sense of the word, and
    how is this meaning applied to the idea of unravelling complications?
    . . . .
12 To 'ease' a confession out of a culprit (line 25) is to . . . .
13 Why does a detective need more skill in the second case than in the first, as
    described in the second paragraph? . . . .
14 'Talking round a subject' (lines 31–32) involves . . . .
15 Contrast the part taken by the detective in interrogating a silent and an over-
    talkative witness or suspect. . . . .
16 In about 100 words give advice to a young detective about how to conduct a
    successful interrogation. . . . .

Section C: Directed Writing

First exercise

A widely-supported proposal has been made to create a new industrial port of
some 80,000 inhabitants by enlarging the existing small fishing port and market
town of Woodchester. The following details are under consideration:

POSITION AND COMMUNICATIONS
  On estuary of River Alvin, about 8 kilometres from sea 200 kilometres from the
  capital

Woodchester on main railway line and about 10 kilometres from motorway

SURROUNDINGS
Large areas of afforestation (conifers) planted during past 25 years
Otherwise arable and dairy farming

INDUSTRIAL, PORT AND EMPLOYMENT POSSIBILITIES
Large-scale development of existing small wood-processing and paper pulp factory
Projects for light engineering, food-processing and boatbuilding developments
River could be deepened to take medium-sized cargo ships and oil tankers. Provision of facilities for passenger-carrying hovercraft to the Continent under consideration
Considerable present unemployment in surrounding villages

The plan is still in the early stages of discussion when you are asked to give a short survey of the situation on a radio news programme. Your talk will last about two minutes and consist of about 210 words in all. You will probably want to include the above facts, using them either to support the case for development or supplementing them with information which shows the scheme to be impractical.

You should begin the talk in the following way:

A report published yesterday puts the case for the development of Woodchester, at present a small fishing port on the estuary of the River Alvin, into a far larger industrial port of some 80,000 inhabitants.
Woodchester is situated ....

Second exercise

The following is a short article appearing in a woman's magazine. Compose an answer to it, expressed in a more formal written style, to appear in the next issue. The first part of your letter summarises briefly the writer's attitude to men and women employers and the second either supports or attacks her arguments, introducing additional material to confirm your case. The beginning of the letter has been written for you: write another 125–190 words.

Fair play for the woman in charge

They say that a lot of women are conservative, without minds of their own and completely prejudiced against their own sex. And how right they seem to be!

How about last week's opinion poll on men and women bosses? How many of you girls favoured the man in charge? Eighty-eight per cent of you!

It beats me! I've met some of these wonderful supermen. So have you, poor things. As soon as he gets in, you see the storm signals: he's in one of his MOODS! Probably a hangover or a row with the wife, a lost contract or just plain nasty temper. Or he's a ditherer who can NEVER make up his mind or spends a whole morning counting the number of paper clips used in the past week. He has 'favourites' like baby, blue-eyed, mentally defective Daphne, who can't stick a stamp on a letter straight; or else all his women staff get the same treatment—as imbeciles to be suffered impatiently. He is either self-satisfied or spineless, dictatorial or incompetent (or both), patronising or remote. How many of the male bosses you've met could you ENDURE as a lifelong partner?

The woman boss starts off with problems: male employees despise her; female ones resent her. She has to be twice as intelligent—and tough—as a man to get the job in the first place. So she is efficient and hard-working. She may expect us to work hard too—and why not?—but she treats us as adult human beings, and with sympathy too when needed. She suppresses whatever 'moods' she may have as bad for staff morale: if you do get the wrong side of her tongue, you probably deserve it. And she is fair.

Can it be, girls, that you're not so emancipated as you imagine? That you actually ENJOY being dominated by an arrogant and/or inefficient lord and master better than being treated as an intelligent equal by one of yourselves?

Madam,

I read with interest your article about the merits and faults of men and women employers. I understand from it that you consider men ....

Third exercise

This is part of a table published a few years ago which provides statistical details based on information obtained from sample groups of British women of various ages.

CHIEF LEISURE ACTIVITIES—FEMALES
Percentage of leisure periods when named activity cited as chief pursuit.

	Single 19–22	Married without children	Married with children	Single 22–31	Single 31–45	Single 46–60	Married over 60	Widowed over 60
Watching television	10	16	24	11	24	23	29	25
Reading	4	7	4	9	7	8	10	13
Crafts and hobbies	13	21	24	11	22	15	14	12
Social activities	7	13	7	7	5	9	6	14
Physical recreation								
(a) as participant	28	10	2	28	1	2	1	—
(b) as spectator	1	2	1	2	1	1	—	—
Excursions, walk etc.	12	13	17	2	15	14	14	7

Prepare a report of between 160 and 190 words based on some of these figures and designed for publication in a sociological journal. Only general tendencies should be dealt with and no figures need to be introduced. The main emphasis in the report will be on the contrasting popularity of certain activities with younger and older age groups and there should be a few suggestions of possible causes of the disparities.

Here is a suitable, though not obligatory, opening:

Figures based on information gathered from sample groups of women of various ages suggest that watching television is very popular with all age groups. Younger single women however ....

4 Listening comprehension

(The passages on which the following questions are based are to be found in the Key to this book, which is published separately.)

Section A: Questions and Responses

You will hear each passage read twice over, and you will be given time to choose your answers to the questions on each passage. Write the number of each question and after it the letter A, B, C or D for the answer you choose. *Give one answer only* to each question.

First passage

1   The main subject of the passage is that most husbands

    A   do not like to go shopping
    B   refuse to have anything to do with shopping
    C   are like children when they go shopping
    D   have false ideas about goods and prices

2   One kind of man is described as a 'boss' husband because

    A   he will help his wife only under exceptional circumstances
    B   he is very bad-tempered while shopping
    C   he insists on certain conditions before going shopping
    D   nothing will make him go shopping

3   The husband who comes shopping only if his wife asks him to do so

    A   makes a fuss about it then and for some time after
    B   feels sorry for her because she has so much to do
    C   wants to return as soon as possible to do some painting
    D   is recognised by his wife as better than most husbands

4   Where did the information in the passage first appear in print?

    A   In a woman's magazine
    B   As a published report on the subject
    C   As a feature article in a newspaper
    D   As a radio programme based on interviews with various women

5   The dilettante husband

    A   never knows what he wants

B behaves in a childish way

C asks for a lot of things which his wife considers unnecessary

D always insists on accompanying his wife shopping

6 How did most of the women interviewed feel about their husband's attitude?

A They found it unacceptable

B They accepted it as justifiable

C They resented it but took it for granted

D They realised that their husbands were too busy to help them

Second passage

1 What happened when Frances reached the door of the garden room?

A She realised the room was empty so decided not to go in

B She turned the handle but did not open the door

C She intended to go in but was too afraid to do so

D She opened the door but lost her nerve and closed it again

2 What were her surroundings like when she came out through the door?

A She was in a street between high buildings

B She was above an enclosed area

C She was standing on a stone-covered area

D She was at the foot of a flight of steps

3 What impression did Frances have of the wind?

A The courtyard was still, though the wind raced round the outer walls

B After its earlier violence it had died down a little

C It roared round the walls like a lion

D It seemed particularly strong within the yard

4 What was the sky like?

A It was entirely covered with heavy clouds

B There was a moon surrounded by clouds

C The moon was shining brightly through passing clouds

D There was very considerable cloud movement

5 As she moved in the near-darkness she was aware of

A a large box behind her

B a small building against the middle of a wall ahead

C a gallery in a corner containing some wood

D an object beside her which had been bought in China

6 What frightened her most about the scene in the garden room was

A the anger on the face of the man inside

B the terrifying sense of unreality about the scene

C her conviction that something terrifying was about to happen

D the alarming change in the appearance of the person she thought she knew

7   What was her reaction to what she saw?

   A   She was too terrified to do anything
   B   She tried to force herself to go into the garden room
   C   She waited a moment and then screamed
   D   She made up her mind to force her way in to the room

Third passage

1   What was Sheridan's opinion of his home?

   A   It was typically English
   B   The house itself had just the qualities he valued
   C   It suited him so well that the noise did not matter
   D   It was just like a home in England would have been

2   What did Emmy do immediately after the meal?

   A   She cleared the table
   B   She washed up
   C   She sat by the fire
   D   She chatted about Sherlock Holmes

3   What kind of work did Johnson do?

   A   He was an actor
   B   He was a playwright
   C   He was a car park attendant
   D   He was a parking inspector

4   What advice did Sheridan give Joe?

   A   Not to pass on what he was being told
   B   To look out for possible danger or trouble
   C   To entrust Sheridan with some information he had
   D   To give close attention to what he was going to be told

5   Sheridan was considering the idea of

   A   investigating some murders
   B   assisting Sherlock Holmes on one of his cases
   C   preparing a T.V. series based on a murder investigation
   D   writing a book about a murder investigation

6   How did Sheridan rate his qualifications for his undertaking?

   A   His acting ability was likely to be useful
   B   He would need information available to a professional investigator
   C   As an amateur he would be hopelessly out-of-date
   D   Although professionally unqualified, he might still produce useful ideas

Fourth passage

1 The light from the café

    A   illuminated a considerable part of the Square
    B   formed a segment of a circle outside the café
    C   was shed by a light outside the café
    D   fell across the Square in a broad beam

2 The shadows of the arcade pillars were created by

    A   moonlight
    B   street lights overhead
    C   lighting from within the arcade
    D   the contrast between the dark pillars and the cobblestones

3 Why did Denning pause near the arch?

    A   He wanted to discover whether he was being followed
    B   He had intended to light a cigarette
    C   This was a suitable observation point
    D   It was a secure hiding-place

4 What impression did the scene around him make during the first few moments?

    A   There was no cause for alarm
    B   What he saw increased his apprehension
    C   Only the parked car suggested possible danger
    D   Despite an apparent normality, danger was lurking

5 The car which crossed the Square

    A   raced across from north to south of the Square
    B   came into the Square as if it were being pursued
    C   was travelling across the Square from north to south
    D   could be seen approaching the Square and disappearing in the opposite direction

6 What impression did Denning have of the passing car?

    A   The driver was on the look-out for somebody
    B   There was something furtive in the way it had approached
    C   There was a sinister explanation for its careful approach
    D   It was in some way involved in the dangerous situation he was anticipating

7 The statement 'Yet people did park their cars in narrow alleys' suggests that

    A   this normal action was the reason for the car's slow approach
    B   a car had been left there for some criminal purpose
    C   this made the presence of a parked car in the square more suspicious
    D   there might have been nothing suspicious in the parking of a car in the narrow street

5 Interview

Section A: Photograph

Photograph 1

Suggested range of questions and topics

1 How does the man on the left spend a lot of his free time, and with what result?

2 What advantages does he get from his hobby?

3 Why is the man on the right laughing?

4 Which of the two houses would you choose to buy or rent, and why?

5 What might be a moral of this picture?

The two houses shown are typical of many in Great Britain. How far do they resemble and how far differ from houses in your own country?

The pleasures and drawbacks of gardening.

Some of the uses of a garden.

An active holiday and a really relaxing one.

The advantages an active and creative hobby may have over a largely passive one, like watching television.

Photograph 2

Suggested range of questions and topics

1   What do you think the boy is saying?

2   Why are the policemen laughing?

3   Suggest a possible reason why the police are standing there.

4   What impression have you of the other people in the picture?

5   Describe the background of the picture.

The main duties of the police.

The usefulness and limitations of policewomen.

The qualities of a good policeman.

The possible effects of a policemen's strike.

127

Photograph 3

Suggested range of questions and topics

1 Why could this be described as a restful picture?

2 What qualities has it as a photograph?

3 What details suggest the woman's age?

4 Suggest what she is knitting and whom she is knitting it for.

Ways in which old people can pass the time enjoyably.

Some of the things that the State and the community in general (voluntary workers and neighbours) can do to make life pleasanter for old people.

Some of the problems of having a very old person in the home—both for the old person and the family.

Some of the advantages of residence in a good Old People's Home.

Section B: Topic

Prepare yourself to speak for 2 minutes on any *one* of the following topics. You may make notes on a separate piece of paper and refer to them during your talk, but you must not write out the complete talk and simply read it aloud.

1 How would you view the prospect of achieving complete weather control by experts?
2 The value or otherwise of nursery school attendance by children of pre-school age.
3 What kind of job would you prefer: with a large firm, a small one or as a self-employed person? Explain your choice.

Section C: Dialogue

Dialogue 1

Prepare yourself to read the part of TREMAYNE.

Florence: I'm not so sure. I'm trying to arrange to go out to the Crimea.
TREMAYNE: How?
Florence: As a nurse!
TREMAYNE: ... But there aren't any nurses, Flo!
Florence: Well, I should be one. And I think I can get funds to take out a couple more.
TREMAYNE: What? Privately?
Florence: Why not?
TREMAYNE: Why not? I never heard of a more hare-brained idea. You'd have no standing. Do you suppose the military authorities are going to have unofficial civilians intruding into their hospitals? They can't! They're under War Office regulation ... The thing's absurd!
Florence: We shall have letters of introduction to the Embassy.
TREMAYNE: Yes, at Constantinople. That's not the seat of war.
Florence: Scutari, where the hospitals are, is only a suburb of Constantinople.
TREMAYNE: But it's under military control, my dear. The Ambassador has no power there. And if he has, do you suppose he'd use it?
Florence: He has special powers from the Government.
TREMAYNE: But he can't override the military authorities! And if he could, he wouldn't for an unknown woman. I'll tell you exactly what he will do. He'll tell his wife to have you to afternoon tea and an evening party or two. And everyone will be charming until you try to do something—and then everyone will freeze, and obstacles will

130

spring up all round you and you'll find yourself faced wherever you look with a blank official wall. . . . Don't think of it, Florence. You'd only succeed in branding yourself as a crank and a nuisance. Do be advised, my dear. Remember I was in the Diplomatic Service for three years. The public departments don't encourage amateurs—especially amateurs who want to get things done and know how to do them.

Florence: I don't care. I believe as firmly as ever in my call to service.

TREMAYNE: There are people who believe the earth is flat, and obstinately persist in doing so in spite of all evidence to the contrary. . . .

Florence: Henry, *you* don't doubt me?

TREMAYNE: Just consider. You've spent all your youth chasing shadows. You've hunted yourself from hospital to hospital. And what have you achieved?

Dialogue 2

Prepare yourself to read the part of GRACE.

Arthur: I know exactly what I'm doing, Grace. I'm going to publish my son's innocence before the world, and for that end I am not prepared to weigh the cost.

GRACE: But the cost may be out of all proportion . . .

Arthur: It may be. That doesn't concern me. I hate heroics, Grace, but you force me to say this. An injustice has been done. I am going to set it right, and there is no sacrifice in the world I am not prepared to make in order to do so.

GRACE: Oh, I wish I could see the sense of it all! He's perfectly happy, at a good school, doing very well. No one need ever have known about Osborne, if you hadn't gone and shouted it out to the whole world. As it is, whatever happens now, he'll go through the rest of his life as the boy in that Winslow case . . . the boy who stole that postal order . . .

Arthur: The boy who didn't steal that postal order.

GRACE: What's the difference? When millions are talking and gossiping about him, a 'did' or a 'didn't' hardly matters. The Winslow boy is bad enough. You talk about sacrificing everything for him; but when he's grown up he won't thank you for it, Arthur . . . even though you've given your life to . . . publish his innocence as you call it. Yes, Arthur . . . your life. You talk gaily about arthritis and a touch of gout and old age and the rest of it, but you know as well as any of the doctors what really is the matter with you. You're destroying yourself, Arthur, and me and your family besides . . . and for what I'd like to know? I've asked you and Kate to tell me a hundred times . . . but you never can. For what, Arthur?

Arthur: For Justice, Grace.

GRACE: That sounds very noble. Are you sure it's true? Are you sure it isn't plain pride and self-importance and sheer brute stubbornness?

Arthur: No, Grace. I don't think it is. I really don't think it is ...

GRACE: No. This time I'm not going to cry and say I'm sorry, and make it all up again. I can stand anything if there is a reason for it. But for no reason at all, it's unfair to ask so much of me. It's unfair. ...

Section D: Situations

1 You have been standing at the counter in a crowded shop for several minutes, waiting to be served. Just as your turn comes, someone who has pushed his or her way to the front speaks first and gets attention. You protest.

2 During your English class you need to blow your nose and discover you have no handkerchief with you. You reluctantly interrupt the lesson. ...

3 You have an appointment with a Mr. A. M. White who works in a large office block. The receptionist sends you to Room 608 but you find nobody there and the name on the door is E. N. White. You return to the receptionist and explain.

4 While asking for information at a railway station you leave your suitcase standing a few yards behind you. On going to pick it up again you discover a case that is very similar to but not your own, and a man or woman is walking away with yours. You follow and explain.

5 In an Underground railway station you put the right money in a ticket machine but get no ticket. You report this to an official.

6 You leave your car in front of a parking meter and go to ask for change for the meter at the only shop opposite. This takes five minutes as the shop is crowded and on your return you find an unfriendly-looking traffic warden just putting a ticket on your windscreen. Explain matters.

7 You are attracted by a recorded song you hear on the radio and write down the title and singer but have no information about the record as a whole. You go into a record shop and ask the assistant to help you.

8 During a brief telephone conversation a relative tells you that he/she is looking forward to seeing a certain film that evening. Having seen the film you know that the relative will dislike it intensely. Attempt to dissuade him or her from going.

9 While you are alone in a students' café, you hear someone in a group at the same table say something about your country that gives a completely false impression (for example, that all shopkeepers are dishonest). You feel you must correct this statement but do so politely.

10 As a businessman in your own country, circumstances force you to cancel a business trip to London. You explain on the telephone why you cannot come and suggest a postponement.

11 You have bought a garment in a large supermarket where there are no

facilities for trying things on. At home you discover the size is not right and suspect the number on the label is wrong so you take it back, explain and ask for a replacement.

12 A holiday hostess is seeing you off at the station. Just before you have to say goodbye, you express your thanks and appreciation.

13 You have taken a holiday job in Britain in order to improve your English but find you have to work so hard that you have almost no opportunity to talk to anybody or to see your surroundings. After a fortnight you explain the situation to your employer.

14 You should be meeting, at the airport, a British friend visiting you for the first time, but at the last minute find this impossible. You arrange for a message to be given to the person at the airport, asking him or her to telephone you at a certain number.

15 You have been involved in a minor road accident; explain to the police what happened.

Stage 3

Examination
Level

Practice papers: A

Paper 1. Composition (3 hours)

Answer questions 1, 2 and 3. You should spend about the same amount of time on each.

Section A

1 **Either** (*a*) You are in a crowded dance hall (or eating in a crowded restaurant) when there is a quite unexpected power failure and all the lights in that area of the town go out. Relate what happens.

   or   (*b*) Chris, aged twenty-five and unmarried, has undertaken three contrasting jobs, each for less than six months and each for the sake of the experience it can provide of life, people, surroundings and working conditions. Describe each of the jobs undertaken, suggesting what Chris (who may be a man or a woman) has learned from it.

2 **Either** (*a*) Suggest some of the probable effects of a falling birth-rate.

   or   (*b*) The advantages of living alone.

Section B

Model questions and answers

3 **Read the following passage and then answer the questions which follow it.**

At first there was nothing—a profound blue darkness running deep, laced by skeins of starlight and pale phosphorescent flashes. This four o'clock hour was a moment of utter silence, the indrawn breath of dark, the absolute, trance-like balance between night and day. Then, when it seemed that nothing
5 would ever move or live or know the light again, a sudden hot wind would run over the invisible water. It was like a fore-blast of the turning world, an intimation that its rocks and seas and surfaces still stirred against the sun. One strained one's eyes, scarce breathing, searching for a sign. Presently it came. Far in the east at last the horizon hardened, an imperceptible line dividing sky
10 and sea, sharp as a diamond cut on glass. A dark bubble of cloud revealed

itself, warmed slowly, flushing from within like a seed growing, a kernel ripening, a clinker hot with a locked-in fire. Gradually the cloud throbbed red with light, then suddenly caught the still unrisen sun and burst like an expanding bomb. Flares and streamers began to fall into the sea, setting all things
15 on fire. After the long unthinking darkness everything now began to happen at once. The stars snapped shut, the sky bled green, vermilion tides ran over the water, the hills around took on the colour of firebrick, and the great sun drew himself at last raw and dripping from the waves. Scarlet, purple and clinker-blue, the morning, smelling of thyme and goats, of charcoal, splintered
20 rock and man's long sojourn around this lake, returned with a calling of dogs, the cough of asses and the hoarse speech of the fishermen going down to the working sea.

Some fishermen, of course, had been there all night, fishing far out with lamps; and now, in the overlapping light of dawn, they returned from the deep
25 water to meet their poorer brothers setting out to fish the inshore shallows. In from the horizon, across the chill, flat, crimson silence, the little fleet came throbbing to the shore. As the vessels grounded, the fishermen of the night sprang red-legged into the water, wading ashore with cries and coughing, while a team of oxen, backing into the waves, hauled each boat up the sands.
30 Then the poor scratch fishermen of the morning took over, setting out in their long curved boats and rowing like madmen across the copper sea. The dark silhouettes of their craft, and of the bent men rowing, looked as old as Greece and revolved against the coloured water like ancient paintings on a pot. A man in the boat's high stern paid out a net, while the crew rowed lustily
35 to his cries, kicking up little flames of spray. A net was laid in an arc offshore, tethered to the land by its separate ends. Then two gangs of short, bandy-legged little men took these ends and began to haul it in again. It was a kind of slave-labour, to be witnessed every morning. Panting, swearing, yelping and groaning, they toiled up the beach, while the heavy net, inch by
40 inch, was laboriously hauled ashore.

(a) Comment on the author's use of contrast applied to the beginning and end of the first paragraph.

He opens the paragraph with a scene of darkness, apparent emptiness and silence, a world without light or life. He concludes it with a description of a world bathed in early morning light and colour, busy with the movement and noise of men and animals.

(b) In what sense is the hot wind mentioned in line 5 'a foreblast of the turning world' (l. 6)?

It is a sign that despite the prevailing darkness a large part of the revolving earth is already being lit and warmed by the sun.

(c) Why is the horizon said to 'harden' (l. 9)?

In darkness there is no distinction between sea and sky but the dividing

138

line between them becomes clear and firm as the sky begins to grow light.

(*d*) What justification is there for terming the darkness 'unthinking' (l. 15)?

The absence of light suggests an absence of consciousness, darkness therefore being considered a time of mere existence without thought.

(*e*) In place of 'The stars disappeared' what additional idea is suggested by the expression 'The stars snapped shut' (l. 16)?

A snapping movement is a single one, one that happens almost instantaneously as in the clicking of a camera shutter. The stars disappeared almost instantaneously.

(*f*) Why should the sun 'draw himself from the water' (l. 18) and not just 'rise'?

'Draw himself' suggests a considerable effort made by an enormous sun emerging slowly from the water.

(*g*) In what sense is the sun 'raw' and 'dripping' (l. 18) as it rises?

'Raw' describes uncooked meat full of blood and is here associated with the redness of the rising sun which may appear to be shedding blood or water as it pulls itself out of the sea.

(*h*) Contrast the writer's use of 'throbbed' in connection with the reddening of the cloud (l. 12) and 'throbbing' in line 27 referring to the approaching fleet.

'Throbbing' is a rhythmic beating vibration. The reddening of the cloud was not continuous but in surges as if blood were being pumped into it. The boats' engines chugged in rhythmic vibration. The first effect is visual, the second auditory.

(*i*) Why should the water kicked up by the oars in line 35 be described as 'little flames of spray'?

The spray lifted or kicked up by the oars was not only the colour of fire in the fire-red light of the rising sun, but the splashes raised may also have resembled flames in their shape.

(*j*) Justify the description of the final paragraph as 'a contrast between a romantic and a realistic view of the inshore fishermen'.

The silhouettes of the curved ships moving over the sea suggest a far distant past with a resemblance in shape and colour to pictures on ancient pots, but we are made very much aware of the strenuous and painful effort and harsh cries of the men hauling in the net.

3 **Read the following passage, and then answer the questions which follow it.**

All cars must have working horns, so the law decrees. Why is this so?

One is presented with an image of a driver coming across some children, happily kicking a ball across the road. The driver sounds his horn, and the children scuttle away, the implication being that more lives have been saved
5   by that wonderful invention, the motor horn.

Frankly, I do not believe it. Motor horn lore has crept its way into our life-style on an assumption, and not a proven fact, that it actually saves lives.

As a timid pedestrian who tends to view traffic as a stream of metal missiles whose object in life is to squash me flat, or achieve a near miss, I view the
10   motor horn with the greatest suspicion.

When the mechanical monster is bearing down on me, and blares its horn for good measure, the effect is either briefly to paralyse me in my tracks, or make me leap into the air, neither of which speeds my exit. It could waste time. Far from being the pedestrian's friend, the horn takes on the guise of an
15   offensive weapon. As buglers used to lead the troops into battle, so the motor horn leads the car.

There are so many research projects whose object appears to be proving the obvious, but why no research into whether the inclusion of a horn in a motor vehicle acts as intended?
20   'We have not done any work on it here,' a spokesman for the Road Research Laboratory, Crowthorne, Berks, said. 'I think there was some done in America on different notes and tones. Have you tried the Home Office?'

'We do have a project to try to make police motor horns more effective on motorways,' the Home Office rejoined. 'But not private cars. Have you tried
25   the Road Research Laboratory?' ...

For the past fortnight, I have been doing my own bit of research by noting occasions when a vehicle has been hooting its horn. There was the occasion when I tried to cross to a traffic island in the middle of Fleet Street. A taxi driver drove towards me, resolutely blaring his horn. For what purpose?
30   There was a traffic jam a few yards further up the road, so it would not have impeded his journey to slow down and let me cross in peace.

During a lift home that evening, a speed merchant nipped up the wrong side of the road to jump the queue at the lights. More horn blaring, because the traffic had started to come towards him from the other direction, and he
35   wanted someone to let him back into the original queue.

The most horrifying piece of horn blowing came on the M6, when I was driving North at a steady 60 mph in the middle lane, doing a petrol conservation stint in a small car. Up loomed a juggernaut container lorry from behind, travelling at speed, blaring its horn non-stop for what seemed like an age, until
40   it was so close that it seemed only a matter of seconds before it would roll right over us. The slow lane was full. The car in front was doing the same speed as we were, and the fast lane was full. There was no alternative but to stay in the lane at the same speed. By the time the situation was resolved, I was shaking like a leaf, and longing to rip out the offending motor horn and
45   stuff it down the driver's throat. These are not emotions which should be engendered by a so-called life-saving device.

140

I would contend that the motor horn is more frequently abused than it is used.

(a) Explain the relationship between the first two paragraphs and what follows them.
(b) What impression of the way motor horn lore has come to be accepted, is conveyed by the words: 'has crept its way into our life style' (lines 6–7)?
(c) Justify the description of traffic as 'a stream of metal missiles' (lines 8–9).
(d) What impression of the advancing car is given that justifies the paralysing effect it has?
(e) What impression of the writer's reception at the two research institutes is conveyed by the last sentence of each of the two paragraphs dealing with them?
(f) Suggest why the writer has used the word 'blaring' rather than 'sounding' line 29?
(g) Explain the special effectiveness of the verb 'loomed' in line 38.
(h) Comment on the effectiveness of the final sentence as related to the opening one.

Paper 2. Reading comprehension (1¼ hours)

Section A

In this section you must choose the word or phrase which best completes each sentence. Write the number of each sentence and after it the letter A, B, C, D or E for the answer you choose. *Give one answer only* to each question.

1 The tools had been loosely packed in the boot of the car and we could hear them _____ as we drove along the rough track.
   A jerking   B jolting   C tossing   D vibrating   E rolling

2 The medicine was so _____ that he was almost back to normal within a few days.
   A efficient   B effective   C competent   D proficient
   E influential

3 You could _____ all the worthwhile information in this book into a few pages.
   A condense   B shorten   C decrease   D minimise
   E contract

4 Several of the off-shore islands are _____ now that we have a motor-boat.
   A available   B accessible   C obtainable   D feasible
   E convenient

5 This paper intends fearlessly to _____ all forms of corruption and falsehood in public life.
   A reveal   B unveil   C uncover   D expose   E disclose

6 The rabbit _____ a few shreds from the lettuce leaf but was clearly not hungry.
   A chewed   B gobbled   C gnawed   D licked   E nibbled

7 He feels slightly _____ but this is a common after-effect of influenza.
   A oppressed   B deprived   C depressed   D dejected
   E repressed

8 The two countries will restore full diplomatic relations now that they have _____ their long-standing border dispute.
   A tackled   B dissolved   C settled   D decided   E concluded

9 Since his _____ as a priest he has been training for missionary work.
   A ordination   B confirmation   C ceremony   D election
   E qualification

10 All the condemned men were _____ a few hours before their intended execution, but they would have to undergo life imprisonment.
   A forgiven   B released   C acquitted   D pardoned
   E reprieved

11 In most of the pre-election speeches a lot of attention was given to the coun-

try's _____ situation.

A economic   B industrious   C commercial   D economical
E monetary

12 The cat _____ herself into a ball and promptly went to sleep.
A curved   B twisted   C wound   D coiled   E curled

13 It takes twenty men two whole days to clear away the _____ left on the beach by holidaymakers on a fine Sunday.
A trash   B debris   C litter   D lumber   E remnants

14 His secretary was amazingly efficient, as near _____ as a human being can be.
A unmistakable   B infallible   C meticulous   D incorrigible
E matchless

15 The new system will have to be _____ carefully over a period before it is applied generally.
A confirmed   B proved   C experimented   D ascertained
E tested

16 He was a kindly old man with a lively intelligence and his many _____ remarks were enjoyed by the company.
A laughable   B facetious   C witty   D merry   E malicious

17 He spends most of his time busily _____ about in his garden and in his workshop.
A pottering   B dawdling   C loitering   D dabbling   E idling

18 He goes to work by bicycle as the local bus service is far from _____.
A reliable   B trustworthy   C assured   D certain
E dependent

19 The _____ which must be followed at all stages of a Parliamentary election has changed little over a long period.
A process   B procedure   C proceeds   D progress   E policy

20 Robinson Crusoe was able to survive on his desert island because he was extremely _____ .
A original   B creative   C resourceful   D flexible
E experienced

21 Our guests didn't turn up so we needn't have bought all that extra food _____.
A on that account   B for all that   C after all   D in that case
E at all events

22 Next month our society will have the honour of a visit by the _____ author, Heathcliffe Rochester.
A notorious   B reputable   C notable   D noteworthy
E celebrated

23 The street was packed with people, trucks and tractors, all there to
_____ the attempt to demolish the beautiful sixteenth-century cottage.
A cancel **B** obstruct **C** counter **D** disregard
E counteract

24 The firm has provided sports fields, tennis courts, a swimming-pool and other
forms of _____ for its employees.
A amusement **B** entertainment **C** diversion **D** recreation
E pleasure

25 The heavy clouds began to withdraw and there was a faint _____ of light
from the stars as they began to appear.
A glimmer **B** flicker **C** sparkle **D** glare **E** glow

26 The faint sound of _____ movements in the kitchen suggested that the
children were secretly helping themselves to the chocolate cake.
A superficial **B** superfluous **C** superstitious **D** supernatural
E surreptitious

27 We shall _____ accept the highest offer though our final decision must de-
pend on the approval of our subsidiary companies.
A eventually **B** presumably **C** admittedly **D** potentially
E ultimately

28 The library which he endowed so generously is one of the many
_____ memorials of his service to the community.
A enduring **B** eternal **C** unending **D** everlasting
E incessant

29 If you have a new key cut, it must be an exact _____ of the existing one.
A duplicate **B** counterfeit **C** model **D** imitation
E reproduction

30 His habit of occasionally talking to himself may seem _____ but it is cer-
tainly no sign of approaching insanity.
A foolish **B** unconventional **C** grotesque **D** eccentric
E awkward

31 The room could have been pleasant but with layers of dust and cobwebs,
torn curtains and broken furniture it looked merely _____.
A gloomy **B** squalid **C** dowdy **D** dismal **E** tawdry

32 It is impossible to _____ the full value of his contribution to human
welfare.
A underrate **B** appreciate **C** assess **D** judge **E** esteem

33 From the beginning of next year the Government will reduce considerably
the _____ paid to dairy farmers.
A donations **B** subscriptions **C** contributions **D** subsidies
E gratuities

34 Your parents will have to give their _____ to your joining the school
gliding club.
A accession **B** ascent **C** access **D** accent **E** assent

35 His influence over union members has _____ since his failure to negotiate higher wages for them.

A deteriorated   B subsided   C declined   D depreciated
E lowered

36 He made an almost _____ movement to signify his agreement.

A unnoticeable   B imperceptible   C invisible   D unseen
E inconspicuous

37 He would not be so overworked if only he would _____ some of his responsibility to his second-in-command.

A delegate   B share   C refer   D consign   E pass over

38 So great had been the shock that his efforts to communicate the information were almost _____ .

A disjointed   B ineligible   C incoherent   D illegible
E intelligible

39 This powder will _____ mice, rats and other vermin from any building.

A obliterate   B exterminate   C suppress   D dispel
E devastate

40 Let us pay tribute to a truly _____ woman: artist, writer and humanitarian.

A conspicuous   B distinguished   C prominent   D notable
E foremost

Section B

In this section you will find after each of the passages a number of questions or unfinished statements about the passage, each with four suggested answers or ways of finishing them. You must choose the one which you think fits best. Write the number of each question and after it the letter A, B, C or D for the answer you choose. *Give one answer only* to each question.
Read each passage right through before choosing your answers.

First passage

Indoors, leisure time was occupied in reading or 'listening-in' to the radio; only a very small number of men indulged in specialist hobbies such as stamp-collecting or model railways. The 'do-it-yourself' home decorations and repairs so widespread today were virtually unknown, for new houses
5 required very little attention of this sort, and when they did, there were usually plenty of professionals available to put things right at modest cost. Such men often remained behind after taking part in the original building work, setting up one-man businesses operating at low profit margins. In the early thirties, a full redecoration of the exterior of a medium-sized semi-detached house could
10 be had for less than £5, a revarnishing of the front door might cost four or five shillings.

An important activity in the first year or so after moving in was the display of the new house to admiring relatives and friends, a ritual usually performed on Sunday afternoons. Supplied with the names of road and house on a
15 letterhead printed at cut price by the newly-established local stationer, the tourists would find themselves veering around the maze of rutted builder's roads, stepping between piles of bricks and prefabricated window frames, trying not to trip over the plankways used for running wheelbarrows between the dumps of materials at the roadside and the building plots. In vain would
20 they make enquiries about their destination from the equally disoriented and widely-scattered inhabitants of the new estate busily clearing their front gardens. Eventually the bright and clean new semi would be found, stark and clinical in its treeless shrubless setting, a carpet of browning turf beneath its proud window bays.
25 Once the ladies of the party had placed their coats on the best bed and rearranged their hair in the mirror of the Drage's or Times Furnishing dressing-table, the first item was a tour of the gardens. Any plants that the new residents had encouraged into sustained life would be meticulously indicated, and the phrase 'a great deal to do yet' was heard more than once.
30 During the walk towards the back fence, the boast would be made, 'they can't build at the back of us', accompanied by a sweep of the arm towards distant woods and meadows precariously glimpsed between other houses. Next came the internal tour, accomplished quickly enough, accompanied by much wall-banging and floor-stamping to emphasise the soundness of construction
35 (politely the visitors would pretend not to notice that the furniture wobbled somewhat during these demonstrations).

Inspection completed, a large tea would be taken: cold meats, or tinned salmon and lettuce followed by many many cakes, sponges and tarts, with perhaps some jelly, trifle or blancmange; a meal so lavish that the whole
40 family would be on a restricted diet for days afterwards to establish financial equilibrium. Afterwards the party would move into the sitting-room for a demonstration of the new radio. This was soon made to interrupt the ripple of feminine chat with snatches of symphonies, jazz, contraltos and sopranos, inter-mixed with a great gibberish of foreign tongues, all to the proud owner's shouts of
45 'That's Berlin', 'Here's Hilversum' or simply, 'Beromunster'.

A couple of hours after tea, as conversation flagged and the guests talked of leaving, they were invited to return to the dinning-room for a second, almost equally enormous meal, washed down with coffee instead of tea. By now it might well be raining; there was no bus, and the muddy trudge through
50 roads lit only by the occasional uncurtained window was sufficiently prolonged by navigational difficulties to ensure that the selected train was missed.

1 Stamp-collecting and model railways

    A   were not really leisure-time occupations

B were among the more unusual of the hobbies pursued

C required some relevant knowledge from those interested in them

D were among the more unpopular hobbies

2 House decoration and repairs

A were never necessary in these new houses

B were very seldom undertaken by the householder

C required the skilled attention of professionals

D were the job of the original builders

3 What reason for the display of the house is implied in the passage?

A The owner regarded this as a good way of attracting and entertaining guests

B It was the usual thing to do

C The owner wanted to justify the fact that he had purchased a house

D This was a traditional custom

4 How did the visitors know where the house was?

A Their host and hostess would send this information to them

B They were provided with the address on arrival at the station

C They carried the name and address on a paper slip detached from a letter

D They would apply to one of the local shopkeepers for the address

5 The visitors' journey to the new house could be described as

A bewildering   **B** exciting   **C** doubtful   **D** distracting

6 What impression is given of the people encountered by the visitors?

A They had little idea of where they were themselves

B They clearly felt confused and depressed

C They were removing abandoned building materials from around their houses

D They were unable to provide help for the visitors

7 What was demonstrated by the host's behaviour during the inspection of the house interior?

A The furniture was less strongly constructed than the house itself

B The house was built in such a way as to minimise noise

C The house was not so solidly built as the owner would have liked to believe

D The construction of the house was very satisfactory

8 An enormous tea was consumed despite the fact that

A nobody would have much appetite for the next few days after it

B the family could ill afford to offer such generous hospitality

C having borrowed money to provide it, the family would have to economise on food afterwards

D the next few meals would be limited to the remains of the tea for purposes of economy

9　Why did the owner of the radio turn to so many different stations?

    A He was anxious to show how many different languages he understood

    B He intended to demonstrate how good the set was

    C He wanted to drown the sound of the women's voices

    D He was trying to locate the station he wanted

10　Why did the visitors miss their train?

    A They were unable to find their way to the station

    B It was impossible to find the station in the rain and darkness

    C They were delayed by a combination of adverse circumstances

    D There was no available transport so they had to walk along dark muddy roads

Second passage

HMS Renown, Britain's second Polaris submarine, returns to the Clyde this week—after 60 days submerged on her eighth operational patrol. Many of her crew, when they come out of the hatch, will feel distate at smelling the fresh breeze of the Gareloch instead of the ship's air conditioning, and will be
5　unable to focus on colours and distances which have been completely absent from the grey enclosed world they have inhabited so much of this summer. Indeed, their eyesight is so unused to distances beyond five or six feet, that sailors have been warned not to drive their cars for some days ashore, after a number of crashes occurred after the patrols.
10　　Their only link with the outside world since the end of June has been a skimpy news bulletin each day and a weekly 'family-gram' from their wives of up to 40 anodyne words, censored by the shore authorities before they receive it. The censorship erases any item which is likely to make them unstable or depressed while on patrol.
15　　Renown's crew is really the only wasting asset in the entire weapon system. Now that submarines have nuclear power units they have an unlimited endurance, since they no longer need to surface frequently like conventional submarines, to recharge their batteries. Their nuclear fuel lasts for about three years. So it is human frailty which puts limits on the submarine's endurance.
20　It is human appetites which eat their way through the carefully packed deep freeze until supplies run out (in fact Renown carries 30 days' extra supplies in case there is an international crisis which causes a sudden extension beyond the 60 days). It is the human mentality which would probably snap first, if the patrols were any longer.
25　　Obviously the technical systems are not infallible. On board there are frequent alarms and emergency drills—some for exercise purposes, some genuine. However, the prevailing impression one gets within the cigar-shaped hull several hundred feet below the surface is that the only variable element in the system, the only vulnerable or remotely unpredictable factor in a Polaris

30 submarine, are the 150 men who make up the crew. Yet everything about
their circumstances conspires to reduce this human volatility to non-
existence.

Shortly before Renown sailed on this patrol I spent seven days at sea in her
under the North Atlantic, accompanied by a Yorkshire Television camera
35 team. Seven days under the ocean might be thought to induce an
overwhelming sense of claustrophobia in those not used to prolonged
enclosure and submersion. This is not so. Renown is no ordinary submarine,
since she is 7,000 tons large, and her dimensions feel roughly comparable to
those of the lower decks of a cross-channel steamer. There is room to move
40 about in a way undreamt of in most other submarines.

Nevertheless, there remains a very strong impression of enclosure, which is
perhaps more psychological than physical. It is a tight little world—of contracting horizons, of little variety or colour, suffused with an antiseptic at-
mosphere of efficiency and mechanised ritual which must have a limiting
45 effect on its denizens. Imagination stays ashore. As the physical world con-
tracts, so, it seems, do the crew's mental and physical requirements. There are
bicycling machines on board but little organised exercise is taken. One inhales
more oxygen and carbon dioxide than is normal, which seems to help
everyone adjust to the fairly unimaginative routine of sleeping, watchkeeping
50 and eating.

1 One thing the Renown crew may not appreciate much on landing is

  A the coldness of the air
  B the smell at Gareloch
  C the change in the quality of the air
  D the force of the wind

2 The men are likely to have difficulty in

  A seeing anything at all more than six feet from them
  B distinguishing between colours
  C finding their way
  D estimating how far away things are from them

3 The men's letters from home are censored because

  A of the possible effect of their contents on the men's work
  B the crew are engaged in highly secret work
  C this is normal procedure in the submarine service
  D they must be kept short

4 The difference between the submarine equipment and the crew referred to in
the third paragraph is that

  A the equipment can endure worse conditions than the men
  B the equipment can stay underwater longer than the men
  C the equipment needs no attention but the men need a good deal
  D the men need more food than the submarine needs fuel

5   The presence of the human crew has the result that

  A   the submarine cannot stay under water for more than 60 days
  B   the submarine must return home every so often
  C   the submarine cannot be operated under water for more than a certain period
  D   the submarine is more likely to develop technical faults after a time

6   What might happen if the submarine patrol continued longer than normal?

  A   There might be various psychological problems among the crew
  B   This would lead to cases of severe mental disturbance
  C   There would be outbreaks of violence
  D   The crew would no longer be able to operate the submarine

7   The emergency drills carried out

  A   could be due to a sudden emergency
  B   are only practice for an emergency
  C   result from an unexpected breakdown in the technical system
  D   take place more often than in other types of submarine

8   What impression do visitors get of the Polaris crew?

  A   Their behaviour is unpredictable
  B   There is considerable variety in the types of crews
  C   Psychologically they suffer no ill-effects from restricted living conditions
  D   They suffer from constant boredom

9   The passage implies that a feeling of claustrophobia in an ordinary submarine might be produced by

  A   breathing air that has been conditioned
  B   a small space in which to live
  C   uncomfortable living conditions
  D   the constant strain on the men's nerves

10   What effect does the life aboard have on the crew?

  A   They become adjusted to a more passive and limited existence
  B   They lose all interest in life
  C   They look forward only to sleeping and eating
  D   They are always dreaming about life ashore

Paper 3. Use of English (3 hours)

Answer all questions

Section A

1 **Fill each of the numbered blanks in the passage with *one* suitable word.**

25th September, 19—

Dear Mr. Hollybush,

Thank you for your letter of the 18th September, which seems to have been _____(1) in the post, as I have only just received it _____ (2) morning.

I am very_____ (3) in your suggestion that I_____ (4) visit your Leicester factory during the _____(5) week and also_____(6) the opening ceremony of your new works_____(7) the East Coast of Scotland on the 8th November.

I should certainly like to_____(8) your_____(9) to visit your Leicester factory, but _____(10) that I shall be _____(11) to be present at the opening ceremony as I shall be taking_____(12) in a business conference in Switzerland on that day. I should however be pleased to have the _____(13) of visiting the new works_____(14) is most convenient to you after my return.

I have discussed with my co-directors your assurance that you will continue to supply us_____ (15) spare_____ (16) even in the_____ (17) of your ceasing to produce the Lynx scooter Model A, but they agree with me in regretting the possible disappearance of this popular model.

I shall telephone in two_____(18) time, that is to say, on the 27th, about my forthcoming visit, and I am looking forward to_____ (19) you next week.

Yours_____(20),

Bruce Brent

2 **Finish each of the following sentences in such a way that it means exactly the same as the sentence printed before it.**

Example: He wasn't at all annoyed by my criticism, which, he said, he found very helpful.

Far . . . .

Answer: Far from being annoyed by my criticism, he said he found it very helpful.

1 This has nothing to do with the case we are considering.

This is quite . . . .

2 There is a danger that you will get a serious illness if you drink this water.
You are running . . . .

3 In spite of his illness he attended the memorial service.
Ill . . . .

4 Everybody must wear a seat belt.
Wearing . . . .

5 The family was living in a converted bus standing in the middle of a field.
The family was living in a bus which . . . .

6 I have a strong feeling that he has spent some time in prison.
I suspect him . . . .

7 Permission for the local residents to use the path as a short cut was taken for granted.
It was taken . . . .

8 They haven't enough time to cover the basic syllabus let alone do background reading.
Doing background reading is out . . . .

9 How loudly he always speaks!
What . . . .

10 He had undergone a very large number of operations.
He had been . . . .

3 **Fill each of the numbered blanks with *one* suitable word or phrase.**
Example: At first they did not believe my story and it took a long time to convince . . . .
Answer: them that it was true/them of the truth of it.

1 When my secretary turned up this morning, she looked so ill that there was nothing I could do but . . . .

2 There's extra milk for you in the refrigerator should . . . .

3 This trunk is too heavy for us to lift. If only George were here. He's so strong that he . . . . .easily.

4 I was able to assemble the parts myself, once I . . . . .instructions carefully.

5 Don't worry. If there had been any change for the worse in Martin's condition, the hospital . . . .

6 You didn't tell me the shops would be closed today. I wish you
. . . .

7 The next person to report a theft was a cyclist whose . . . .

8 The sun was shining so brightly that it appeared to be a warm day, but when I went out I was surprised at how . . . .

4 **For each of the sentences below, write a new sentence *as similar as possible in meaning to the original sentence*, but using the word given in capital letters.**
Example: The performance was not so good as I had anticipated.
EXPECTATIONS
Answer: The performance did not come up to my expectations.

1 The doctor told his overweight patient that he would feel better if he ate less.
RECOMMENDED

2 The suspect assured them that telling them a lie would be impossible for him.
INCAPABLE

3 His study of psychology caused a very great change in his outlook on life.
INFLUENCED

4 He heard only a week later about the birth of this son.
BORN

5 I think it is a great pity you didn't tell me before.
WISH

6 He has not only written the words of the songs but he has also set some of them to music.
BESIDES

7 You should try to be more careful when you type.
MISTAKES

8 It would have been necessary for me to postpone my journey if there had been a strike.
I

9 Please change this pound note for me.
WONDER

10 I felt so full of self-pity that I could take little interest in life.
SORRY

Section B

5 **Read the following passage, and then answer the questions which follow it.**

Granted then, that things do get buried in one or other of these ways, how, it may be asked, do you set to work to find them? Why do you dig just where you do?

Burial does not always mean obliteration, and there are generally some sur-
5 face signs to guide the digger. In the Near East no one could possibly mistake the great mounds or 'tells' which rose above the plain to mark the sites of ancient cities; very often, if the place was an important one, it can be identified from literary sources even before excavation begins; the difficulty is rather, which point of attack to choose in so great an area. In Mesopotamia the

153

10 highest mound will probably conceal the Ziggurat or staged tower attached to
the chief temple; sometimes a low-lying patch will betray the position of the
temple itself. Herodotus, visiting Egypt in the fifth century B.C., remarked
that the temples there always lay in a hollow; the reason was that while the
mud-brick houses of the town were shortlived and new buildings constructed
15 over the ruins of the old quickly raised the ground-level, the temples, built of
stone and kept always in good repair, outlived many generations and
remained at the same level throughout; on an Egyptian site, therefore, a
square depression ringed about by mounds of crumbling grey brick gives the
excavator a very obvious clue. Earthworks are enduring things, and the site,
20 for instance, of a Roman camp in Britain can nearly always be traced by the
low grass-clad lines of its ramparts, and the round barrows of the old British
dead are still clear to see upon the Downs; but even where there is nothing up-
standing, surface indications may not be lacking. In a dry summer the grass
withers more quickly where the soil lies thin over the buried tops of stone
25 walls, and I have seen the entire plan of a Roman villa spread out before me
where no spade had ever dug; darker lines in a field of growing corn or, in the
very early morning, a difference of tone given by the dew on the blades, will
show where buildings run underground: nowadays air photographs bring to
light masses of evidence invisible to one who stands upon the ground. An air
30 photograph gives us the whole layout of the Roman village of Caistor, so that
the excavator can confidently select the particular building he would like to
dig, whereas, before, the site of Caistor was unknown; even more remarkable
is it that an air photograph discovered Woodhenge, and showed on the plain
surface of ploughed fields the concentric rings of dots where thousands of
35 years ago wooden posts had been planted. From the ground such things are
often quite invisible, or visible only at some lucky moment. At Wadi Halfa, in
the northern Sudan, MacIver and I had dug a temple and part of the Egyptian
town, but, search the desert as we might for two months, we had failed to find
any trace of the cemetery which must have been attached to the place. One
40 evening we climbed a little hill behind the house to watch the sunset over the
Nile; we were grumbling at our ill luck when suddenly MacIver pointed to the
plain at our feet; its whole surface was dotted with dark circles which, though
we had tramped over it day after day, we had never seen. I ran down the hill
and the circles vanished as I came close to them, but, guided by MacIver
45 from above, I made little piles of gravel here and there, one in the middle of
each ring; and when we started digging there next morning our Arab
workmen found under each pile the square, rock-cut shaft of a tomb.

1 Suggest a title, based on material in the first paragraph, that might suitably
be given to this passage if it appeared as an article in an archaeological journal . . . .

2 The word 'Granted' in line 1 could be replaced by the words
. . . .

3 Express the last sentence in the first paragraph in another way without using

such pronouns as 'you,' 'one,' or 'we' . . . .

4　In what sense might one 'mistake' the great mounds mentioned in line 6?
　　. . . . .

5　The place 'can be identified from literary sources' (lines 7–8) means that
　　. . . . .

6　A 'point of attack' (line 9) is a place . . . .

7　What is the literal meaning of 'betray' (line 11) and how can this meaning
　　be applied in the present case? . . . .

8　The word 'outlived' in line 16 can be replaced by the words . . . .

9　Add two or three words, to explain the word 'throughout,' to the statement in
　　lines 16–17 'and remained at the same level throughout' . . . .

10　'a square depression' . . . 'gives the excavator a very obvious clue' (lines 17–19)
　　to . . . .

11　Explain in your own words why the grass should wither more quickly in
　　places (lines 23–24) . . . .

12　One word that could exactly replace 'bring to light' in lines 28–29 is
　　. . . . .

13　Who is being referred to by the word 'us' in line 30? . . . .

14　The concentric rings on the air photograph of Woodhenge (line 34) showed that
　　Woodhenge was inhabited long ago because . . . .

15　'Search the desert as we might' (line 38) can be expressed in fairly similar
　　words as . . . .

16　Explain why 'the circles vanished' (line 44) as the writer approached them
　　. . . . .

17　Explain in about 100 words the methods described in the passage for
　　locating the site of a possible worthwhile excavation . . . .

Section C

6 Here is a report prepared by Detective Inspector Ferret, following an interview
with Mr. Peveril Playce and his wife.

Rewrite the passage in the form of a dialogue, giving the words used by each of
the people involved: Ferret, Playce and Mrs. Playce.

Various features of the report which suggest how the person spoke should be
embodied as far as possible in the words used, together with normal speech
abbreviations.

The beginning of the dialogue has been written for you below.

When I called at the flat, a women, apparently Mrs. Playce, opened the door.

Having greeted her, I asked politely if Mr. Peveril Playce lived there. She hesitated, started to answer in the negative, broke off and asked abruptly who I was and what I wanted. I told her who I was, said that I knew Playce lived there and was at home and requested a little sharply that I might see him.

Playce appeared then, said who he was and demanded to know what I wanted. I asked him politely where he had been at half past two that afternoon. He said he had been working and added a sarcastic remark. I asked when he had last seen Matthew Muddle. He appeared to be amazed at the question and finally declared that he had not seen Muddle for two years.

I told him that he had been seen with Muddle at two o'clock that afternoon. He affected incomprehension of my statement at first and with some exasperation asked why I was interested. I explained that Muddle had named him in establishing an alibi for two thirty.

Playce showed relief when he heard this and admitted in a jocular way that he had given Muddle a lift in his lorry to Barnet but had not wanted to admit this as his firm had strict rules about giving lifts. I asked him if he was willing to sign a statement to this effect. He was clearly reluctant to do so but finally unwillingly agreed.

FERRET: Good evening. Would you mind telling me if Mr. Peveril Playce lives here?

MRS. PLAYCE: Oh, er . . . No, he . . . Anyhow, just who are you? What do you want?

FERRET: ....

Paper 4. Listening comprehension (30 minutes)

(The passages on which the following questions are based are to be found in the Key to this book, which is published separately.)

Questions

You will hear each passage read twice over, and you will be given time to choose your answers to the five questions on each passage. Write the number of each question and after it the letter A, B, C or D for the answer you choose. *Give one answer only* to each question.

First passage

1 The main impression given by Garbin's study was one of

    A   discomfort
    B   darkness
    C   shadow
    D   squalor

2 The passage makes it quite clear that the following was/were not new:
    A   the carpet
    B   the armchairs
    C   the wall covering
    D   the bookcases

3 The identity of the person represented by the bust was not clear mainly because of

    A   its position
    B   the difficulty of seeing it
    C   the poor quality of the carving
    D   the fact that it was very old

4 Geoffrey's reaction to the raven was one of

    A   considerable distaste
    B   sudden fear
    C   unexpected horror
    D   momentary disbelief

5 What was Garbin's attitude to his pet?

    A   He felt sorry for it
    B   He had done everything he could to drive it away
    C   It was a sign of his own unusual taste
    D   He had no particular regard for it

Second passage

1 Parkinson's Law can be otherwise explained as

    A   there is never enough time for all the work there is to do

    B   the longer the time available for a job, the longer the job will take

    C   if more time is available, we can always find extra jobs to fill it

    D   if we had more time, we could do more work

2 What is characteristic of the industrialists the writer knows?

    A   They never feel that they work hard enough

    B   They put a great deal of effort into their work

    C   They could make far more effective use of their time

    D   They spend too much time enjoying themselves

3 The writer hints that industrialists waste much of their time on inessentials because

    A   they have little organising ability

    B   this is the only way of passing the time they know

    C   they are unwilling to trust other people to be responsible even for trival matters

    D   they are too thorough and conscientious

4 What surprised the writer about the busy and important man he visited?

    A   The man seemed to have nothing to do

    B   He failed to realise how much he was wasting the writer's time

    C   The fact that a man in his position could be interested in such unimportant things

    D   The fact that he ever managed to complete his day's work

5 In what way is it clear that the president of the medium-sized firm differed from the people referred to previously?

    A   His firm was unsuccessful

    B   He gave all his time to doing his job

    C   He managed to get through far more work

    D   He always forced himself to work very hard

Third passage

1 What does the writer do if she meets a dog in the street?

    A   She goes out of her way to avoid it

    B   She runs away from it

    C   She finds a safe place to wait until it disappears

    D   She makes some excuse to turn back

2 What happens to the dog when the writer arrives at the house she is visiting?

    A   He is persuaded to go into the kitchen

    B   He is forcibly removed elsewhere

    C   He is held back so that she can get in safely

    D   His angry barking changes to a cry of pain

3   What effect do the dog's cries have upon his owner?

    A   With some difficulty she manages to ignore them
    B   She asks her guest's permission to let the animal in
    C   She worries about what might be happening to him
    D   She blames the guest for the dog's unhappiness

4   What startles the hostess as the dog enters the room?

    A   His unexpected appearance
    B   His sudden attack on the guest
    C   The noise he makes as he does so
    D   The guest's reaction

5   What does the guest often have to do?

    A   Put up with the dog's enthusiastic greeting
    B   Get out of the house
    C   Shout angrily at the dog
    D   Move away quickly

Paper 5. Interview (12 minutes)

Section A: Photograph

1. Suggested range of questions and topics.

1   Suggest why the subject of this picture might have appealed to the photographer.

2   How does most of the washing near the four women seem to differ from most of what can be seen in the foreground?

3   Describe the part of the building you can see.

4   Suggest why there should be so much washing.

How countrywomen have done their washing in the past.

Modern ways of doing the washing.

How far the statement 'A housewife's work is never done' is true.

Some other unusual subjects for photographs.

Some of the advantages and disadvantages of living in a block of flats.

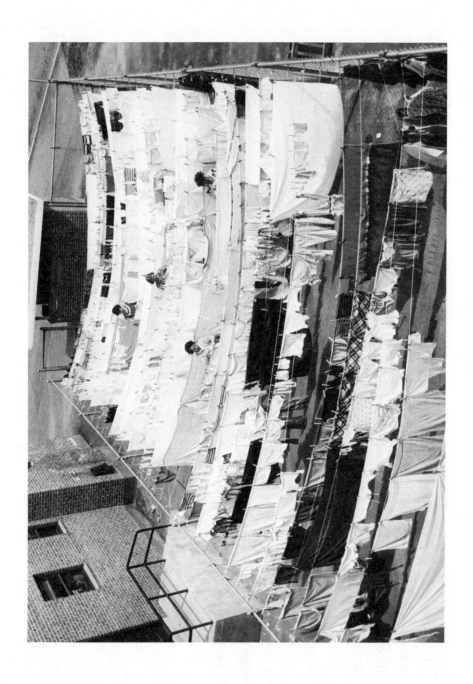

2. *Suggested range of questions and topics*

1 What is this group of people doing? Explain why.

2 Why do most of them look happy?

3 Describe how the two women bridesmaids are dressed.

4 What is the little girl doing? Suggest why.

5 What features of this photograph remind you of a wedding in your country?

6 What differences are suggested?

Your feelings about a quiet wedding as contrasted with an expensive celebration attended by many people.

Another special occasion when a photograph might be taken and what the photograph might show.

The value of marriage.

162

Section B: Topic

Prepare yourself to speak for 2 minutes on any *one* of the following topics. You may make notes on a separate piece of paper and refer to them during your talk, but you must not write out the complete talk and simply read it aloud.

1. The ideal surroundings in which to bring up a family (area, residence, social and other amenities etc.)
2. Your opinion of reports of flying saucers and other forms of influence from 'other worlds'.
3. What can you learn about another person's character from the way he/she drives a car?

Section C: Dialogue

1 Prepare yourself to read the part of CLIVE

Stanley: No, Clive. I told you: I don't understand you at all. Not at all.

CLIVE: You're proud of it too.

Stanley: What now?

CLIVE: That you don't understand me at all. Almost as if it defined you. 'I'm the Man Who Doesn't Understand.' Has it ever occurred to you that *I* don't understand *you*? No. Of course not. Because you're the one who does the understanding around here—or rather fails to. What work did you put in to being able to understand anybody?

Stanley: I think you'd better go to bed.

CLIVE: I'll go to bed when I'm good and ready! ... D'you think it falls into your lap—some sort of grace that enters you when you become a father?

Stanley: You're drunk.

CLIVE: Yes, you think you can treat me like a child—but you don't even know the right way to treat a child. Because a child is private and important and itself. Not an extension of you. Any more than I am. I am myself. Myself. Myself. You think of me only as what I might become. What I might make of myself. But I am myself now—with every breath I take, every blink of the eyelash. The taste of a chestnut or a strawberry on my tongue is me. The smell of my skin is me, the trees and tables that I see with my own eyes are me. You should want to become me and see them as I see them, but we can never exchange. Feelings don't unite us, don't you see? They keep us apart. And words are no good because they're unreal. We live away in our skins from minute to minute, feeling everything quite differently, and any one minute's just as true about us as any other. That's why a question like 'What are you going to be?' just doesn't mean anything at all—. Yes, I'm drunk. You make me drunk.

2 Prepare yourself to read the part of HIGGINS

Liza: I won't care for anybody that doesn't care for me.

HIGGINS: Commercial principles, Eliza. Like selling violets, isn't it?

Liza: Don't sneer at me. It's mean to sneer at me.

HIGGINS: I have never sneered in my life. Sneering doesn't become either the human face or the human soul. I am expressing my righteous contempt for Commercialism. I don't and won't trade in affection. You call me a brute because you couldn't buy a claim on me by fetching my slippers and finding my spectacles. You were a fool: I think a woman fetching a man's slippers is a disgusting sight: did I ever fetch your slippers? I think a good deal more of you for throwing them in my face. No use slaving for me and then saying you want to be cared for: who cares for a slave? If you come back, come back for the sake of good fellowship; for you'll get nothing else. You've had a thousand times as much out of me as I have out of you; and if you dare to set up your little dog's tricks of fetching and carrying slippers against my creation of a Duchess, Eliza, I'll slam the door in your silly face.

Liza: What did you do it for if you didn't care for me?

HIGGINS: Why, because it was my job.

Liza: You never thought of the trouble it would make for me.

HIGGINS: Would the world ever have been made if its maker had been afraid of making trouble? Making life means making trouble. There's only one way of escaping trouble; and that's killing things. Cowards, you notice, are always shrieking to have troublesome people killed.

Section D: Situations

1   You have noticed a person behaving suspiciously outside the house opposite. You know that the people who normally live there are away on holiday so you telephone the police station. Report the circumstances, giving your name and address.

2   You have taken a friend's dog for a walk but the animal disappears. After searching for it for some time, you go back and tell your friend what has happened.

3   You have a sick friend in your car who needs immediate medical attention so you are rushing him/her to hospital. What do you say to the traffic policeman who stops you for speeding?

4   Your neighbour has a dog which is let out every morning and terrifies your own and other children on their way to school. You approach your neighbour on this subject.

5   A passport official is very reluctant to believe that the photograph in your passport is really of you. Try to convince him.

6   You gave in some written work to your teacher a fortnight ago and have not yet had it back. Remind your teacher about it tactfully.

7   Your television set, which is under guarantee, is out of order. Telephone the dealer whom you bought it from, describing what is wrong, asking him for speedy service and reminding him of the guarantee.

8   While you are speaking to your boss on your home telephone, the door bell rings. What do you say to your boss?

9   You telephone an elderly relative who lives alone at about eight o'clock in the evening but get no reply. You are worried because the relative rarely goes out so you telephone a neighbour who has a house key and ask for help.

10 You have taken some medicine prescribed by your doctor but then suffer some very unpleasant effects which you believe have been caused by the medicine. You feel too ill to go out so you telephone the doctor to report the matter. What do you say?

11 You want to finish a telephone call to someone who is so talkative that you cannot get a word in edgeways. Finish the call in a way that can give no offence.

12 You are joining some kind of adventure holiday: rock-climbing, sailing, touring a very remote area in a mini-bus or some other activity that may involve some slight risk. Reassure an elderly relative who is likely to worry about your safety.

13 You have got through on the telephone to a large firm and have asked for a certain extension number. After waiting for two or three minutes without a reply, you hang up and telephone again. Explain to the switchboard operator what has happened.

Practice papers: B

Paper 1. Composition (3 hours)

Answer questions 1, 2 and 3. You should spend about the same amount of time on each.

Section A

1 **Either** (*a*) You are engaged to be married and your fiancé (or fiancée) takes you for the first time to visit his or her parents, who do not approve of the match and have given the invitation reluctantly. Write an account of the visit.

   or

       (*b*) A small group of highly unconventional and experimental painters and sculptors are holding an exhibition of their work wnich you attend. Describe your visit.

2 **Either** (*a*) Some of the possible causes of violence in the world of today and the contrasting forms they may take.

   or   (*b*) The effects that a person's appearance (including clothes) may have on other people and on his or her success in life.

Section B

3 **Read the following passage, and then answer the questions which follow it.**

'Travel' is the name of a modern disease which became rampant in the mid-fifties and is still spreading. The disease—its scientific name is *travelitis furiosus*—is carried by a germ called prosperity. Its symptoms are easily recognisable. The patient grows restless in the early spring and starts rushing
5 about from one travel agent to another collecting useless information about places he does not intend to visit, studying handouts, etc.; then he, or usually she, will do a round of tailors, milliners, summer sales, sports shops and spend three and a half times as much as he or she can afford; finally, in August, the patient will board a plane, train, coach or car and proceed to foreign parts
10 along with thousands of fellow-sufferers not because he is interested in or attracted by the place he is bound for, nor because he can afford to go, but

simply because he cannot afford not to. The disease is highly infectious. Nowadays you catch foreign travel rather as you caught influenza in the twenties, only more so.

15   The result is that in the summer months (and in the last few years also during the winter season) everybody is on the move. In Positano you hear no Italian but only German (for England is not the only victim of the disease); in some French parts you cannot get along unless you speak American; and the official language of the Costa Brava is English. I should not be surprised to

20   see a notice in Blanes or Tossa-de-Mar stating: *Aqui Se Habla Español*—Spanish spoken here.

What is the aim of all this travelling? Each nationality has its own different one. The Americans want to take photographs of themselves: (*a*) in Trafalgar Square with the pigeons, (*b*) in St Mark's Square, Venice, with the pigeons

25   and (*c*) in front of the Arc de Triomphe, in Paris, without pigeons. The idea is simply to collect documentary proof that *they have been there*. The German travels to check up on his guide-books: when he sees that the Ponte di Rialto is really at its proper venue, that the Leaning Tower is in its appointed place

30   and is leaning at the promised angle—he ticks these things off in his guide book and returns home with the gratifying feeling that he has not been swindled. But why do the English travel?

First, because their neighbour does and they have caught the bug from him. Secondly, they used to be taught that travel broadens the mind and

35   although they have by now discovered the sad truth that whatever travel may do to the mind, certain kinds of foreign food certainly broaden other parts of the body, the old notion still lingers on. But lastly—and perhaps mainly—they travel to avoid foreigners. Here, in our cosmopolitan England, one is always exposed to the danger of meeting all sorts of peculiar aliens.

40   Not so on one's journeys in Europe, if one manages things intelligently. I know many English people who travel in groups, stay in hotels where even the staff is English, eat roast beef and Yorkshire pudding on Sundays and Welsh rarebit and steak and kidney pudding on weekdays, all over Europe. The main aim of the Englishman abroad is to meet people; I mean, of course, nice

45   English people from next door or from the next street. Normally one avoids one's neighbour ('It is best to keep yourself to yourself'—'We leave others alone and want to be left alone' etc., etc.). If you meet your next door neighbour in the High Street or at your front door you pretend not to see him or, at best, nod coolly; but if you meet him in Capri or Granada, you embrace

50   him fondly and stand him a drink or two; and you may even discover that he is quite a nice chap after all and both of you might just as well have stayed at home in Chipping Norton.

(*a*)   Explain how the writer catches his reader's attention in the opening sentence.

(*b*)   Comment on his use of the pseudo-Latin expression in lines 2–3.

(*c*)   How appropriate do you consider his reference to the travel disease germ of 'prosperity' (l. 3)?

(*d*) Comment on his use of exaggeration in the second paragraph to convey the extent of foreign travel in Europe.

(*e*) Explain the additional implication in the words 'the old notion still lingers on' (l. 37) as compared with 'the old notion still exists'.

(*f*) Comment on the apparently absurd statement 'They travel to avoid foreigners' (l. 38)

(*g*) What is the origin of the statements in inverted commas and brackets (lines 46–47)?

(*h*) What earlier statement in the same paragraph does the final sentence refer to?

Paper 2. Reading comprehension (1¼ hours)

Section A

In this section you must choose the word or phrase which best completes each sentence. Write the number of each sentence and after it the letter A, B, C, D or E for the answer you choose. *Give one answer only* to each question.

1 The church is famous for its medieval _____ glass windows.
   A coloured   **B** painted   **C** decorated   **D** stained   **E** gilded

2 He fell heavily and was immediately conscious of a(n)_____ pain in his right shoulder.
   A strong   **B** hard   **C** raw   **D** keen   **E** acute

3 Policemen on duty at the football match had to remove spectators who had invaded the_____ in order to stop the game.
   A track   **B** ground   **C** pitch   **D** field   **E** course

4 The prisoners were exercising in the prison yard under the _____ watchful eye.
   A keeper's   **B** warden's   **C** guardian's   **D** warder's
   E sentry's

5 The rock-climbers seemed quite _____ to the dangers of this new method of ascent.
   A unaware   **B** blind   **C** oblivious   **D** accustomed
   E undeterred

6 For the time_____ they are living with relatives, but they are looking for a home of their own.
   A present   **B** existing   **C** being   **D** now   **E** foreseeable

7 You will need a_____ from the police if you want to stay in this country any longer.
   A permit   **B** permission   **C** licence   **D** grant   **E** allowance

8 These scissors are too_____ to cut anything with.
   A serrated   **B** blunt   **C** dull   **D** blurred   **E** numb

9 Anglo-Saxon warriors enjoyed_____ about their battle exploits.
   A gloating   **B** exulting   **C** showing off   **D** bluffing
   E boasting

10 The light was so_____ that it hurt my eyes.
    A intense   **B** shining   **C** opaque   **D** stark   **E** intensive

11 It would have been wiser to _____ the subject as it seemed to be causing offence to some of those present.
    A leave   **B** give over   **C** alter   **D** drop   **E** give up

12 He had a_____ escape when his boat was capsized by a sudden gust of wind.

170

A close   **B** sudden   **C** near   **D** narrow   **E** breathtaking

13   I shall take an earlier train so as to _____ that I won't miss the connection at Crewe.
     A assure   **B** determine   **C** ensure   **D** certify   **E** insure

14   I had little hope of winning the next game as my _____ was an Olympic gold medallist.
     A antagonist   **B** opponent   **C** rival   **D** partner
     E contestant

15   Try to _____ a good example to the newcomers.
     A make   **B** do   **C** provide   **D** set   **E** show

16   The country is in grave danger of being torn apart by _____ war.
     A citizens'   **B** national   **C** partisan   **D** domestic   **E** civil

17   Evening class student numbers fell _____ when the cold weather started.
     A down   **B** away   **C** off   **D** out   **E** back

18   The grave faces of the people, when they heard of the death of their admired leader, showed their _____ at his passing.
     A grievance   **B** bitterness   **C** envy   **D** mourning   **E** grief

19   Put that dog outside. He keeps _____ in my way.
     A getting   **B** coming   **C** passing   **D** being   **E** moving

20   His job is a very _____ one as it involves long hours and demands intense concentration.
     A exhaustive   **B** exact   **C** inflexible   **D** unsparing
     E exacting

21   You're not really fit again yet so you should _____ against overtiring yourself.
     A take care   **B** take measures   **C** provide   **D** guard
     E defend

22   I agree with you to a certain _____ but not entirely.
     A extent   **B** part   **C** way   **D** level   **E** effect

23   He at last _____ his ambition of sailing across the Atlantic.
     A effected   **B** wrought   **C** achieved   **D** performed
     E completed

24   Like the dinosaur, this species is now quite _____ .
     A extant   **B** extinguished   **C** expired   **D** extinct
     E annihilated

25   The example you have just referred to has no _____ on the matter under discussion.
     A relation   **B** connection   **C** relationship   **D** dependence
     E bearing

26 On paper your scheme is excellent, but whether it will be _____ just now will depend on the money available for its realisation.

  A wise **B** sensible **C** practical **D** rational **E** practicable

27 We cannot give you the money until you can show us some form of _____: a passport, driving licence or pension book.

  A identity **B** proof **C** surety **D** identification **E** paper

28 The two countries have broken _____ their negotiations to settle the border dispute.

  A down **B** from **C** off **D** up **E** out

29 Since this make of car went out of production, it has been very difficult to get _____ parts for replacements.

  A auxiliary **B** spare **C** extra **D** supplementary
  E alternative

30 He exaggerates so much that I _____ little importance to anything he says.

  A give **B** subscribe **C** impose **D** attach **E** extend

31 It was clearly _____ to argue any further as he was obviously determined not to co-operate.

  A inconsistent **B** futile **C** meaningless **D** inadequate
  E aimless

32 Needing money urgently, he arranged a _____ on his house, to be repaid in ten years.

  A deposit **B** mortgage **C** lease **D** freehold **E** rental

33 Determined though I was to diet, the rich cream cake proved to be quite _____.

  A appealing **B** irresistible **C** fatal **D** inevitable
  E delicious

34 The two negotiating parties eventually gave up their extreme demands and reached a(n) _____.

  A balance **B** adjustment **C** bargain **D** compromise
  E parity

35 The judge will hear the next _____ after lunch.

  A trial **B** case **C** charge **D** lawsuit **E** prosecution

36 As the door suddenly slammed, everybody gave a(n) _____ start.

  A unexpected **B** responsive **C** inexplicable **D** spontaneous
  E involuntary

37 To the _____ the language of science and higher mathematics often seems like a foreign tongue.

  A novice **B** layman **C** amateur **D** civilian **E** heretic

38 He won't like it if you try to _____ with his plans.

  A interfere **B** influence **C** take a part **D** intervene
  E intrude

39 He was a(n)_____ child who could read and write some time before he
    started school.
    A premature **B** precocious **C** pretentious **D** progressive
    E ingenious

40 His voice was almost _____ as he tried to make himself heard against the
    roar of the machinery.
    A silent **B** imperceptible **C** inaudible **D** suffocated
    E speechless

Section B

In this section you will find after each of the passages a number of questions or
unfinished statements about the passage each with four suggested answers or
ways of finishing it. You must choose the one which you think fits best. Write the
number of each question and after it the letter A, B, C or D for the answer you
choose. *Give one answer only* to each question.
Read each passage right through before choosing your answer.

First passage

The gift of being able to describe a face accurately is a rare one, as every
experienced police officer knows to his cost. As the *Lancet* put it recently:
'When we try to describe faces precisely words fail us, and we resort to Identikit procedures, unless we are competent draughtsmen and can draw what
5 we mean.'

Yet, according to one authority on the subject, 'We can each probably
recognise more than 1,000 faces, the majority of which differ in fine details'.

This, when one comes to think of it, is a tremendous feat. Some faces may
be obvious—because of their beauty, their repulsiveness, their asymmetry, or
10 some prominent feature such as a large nose or a squint, but, over-all, these
are in the minority. Incidentally, symmetrical faces are relatively rare. This
was strikingly brought out in an article published in one of the glossy weeklies
between the wars. This was a series of photographs of well-known public
figures, such as the Prince of Wales, in which the photograph was made up of
15 a straight view of one side of the face plus a mirror image.

If the faces had been symmetrical, of course, these photographs would
have been easily recognisable. As it was, they were virtually unrecognisable,
some (those with marked asymmetry) being totally so.

Curiously enough, relatively little attention has been devoted to the fun-
20 damental problem of how and why we acquire this gift for recognising and
remembering faces. Is it an inborn property of our brains, or an acquired
one? As so often happens, the experts tend to differ.

Thus, some contend that it is inborn, and that there are 'special
characteristics about the brain's ability to distinguish faces'. In support of this
25 thesis they note how much better we are at recognising a face after a single
encounter than we are, for example, in recognising an individual horse. On the
other hand there are those, and they are probably in the majority, who claim

that the gift is an acquired one.

The arguments in favour of this latter view, it must be confessed, are im-
30 pressive. It is a habit that is acquired soon after birth. Watch, for instance,
how a quite young baby recognises his mother by sight. Granted that his
other senses help—the sound of her voice, his sense of smell, the distinctive
way she handles him.

But of all these, sight is predominant. Granted, too, that in the first year or
35 so of life the recognition may fade after a relatively long absence, as not a few
mothers have found to their bitter astonishment; but the visual recognition
soon returns.

Thus engendered at the very beginning of life, the ability to recognise faces
quickly becomes an established habit, and one that is essential for daily living,
40 if not necessarily for survival. How essential and valuable it is we probably do
not appreciate until we encounter people who have been deprived of the
faculty.

This unfortunate inability to recognise familiar faces is a well-known, if
relatively uncommon entity, but such people can often recognise individuals
45 by their voices, their gaits, or their spectacles. Perhaps the most striking
example of this odd condition is that recorded of the man walking in a shop
who saw another approaching him and stood aside to let him pass. The 'man'
proved to be himself in a mirror at the end of the passage, but he had not
recognised himself.

50 With typical human ingenuity many of these unfortunate people overcome
their handicap by recognising other characteristic features.

1   What does an experienced police officer know about the ability to describe
    faces?
    A   Few people can give exact details of the appearance of a face
    B   It is unusual for a person to be able to identify a face satisfactorily
    C   The ability to recognise faces unhesitatingly is an unusual gift
    D   Only a few people can visualise faces they have seen

2   When does this large-scale recognition seem a tremendous feat?
    A   Only when one considers it deeply
    B   When one reflects on what is normally taken for granted
    C   When one considers all its possibilities
    D   When one considers the various types of ability it involves

3   Our ability to recognise so many faces is surprising because
    A   most faces are basically rather similar
    B   it involves an enormous feat of memory
    C   it has never been satisfactorily explained
    D   there is such a variety of facial peculiarities

4   The new faces shown were virtually unrecognisable because
    A   they were no longer symmetrical
    B   the two sides had changed their relative positions

C one side of each face was no longer the same

D the two sides of each face had been reversed and changed

5 Some of the faces shown in the photographs

    A were unlike those of the original subject in every way

    B had nothing in common with the face of the person photographed

    C had the two parts of the face reversed

    D changed the person's appearance so much as to make identification impossible

6 What does the writer find strange about an ability to recognise and remember faces?

    A That we do not know more about it

    B That so little use has been made of it

    C That so little research has been carried out into its nature

    D That so little has been discovered about its development and function

7 What is the first suggested explanation of the origin of this ability?

    A It is one of the characteristics peculiar to human beings

    B We are taught it as babies

    C It is learned from our environment and experiences

    D It is something we can do from the moment we are born

8 The idea following the words 'Granted that . . .' in line 34

    A is to be taken for granted

    B is an exception to the preceding statement

    C suggests that the preceding statement may need some modification

    D is an additional idea supporting what has gone before

9 According to the passage, how important is the ability to recognise faces?

    A It is useful in daily life but is not indispensable to it

    B Its absence will make normal everyday life impossible

    C Under certain circumstances we could not exist without it

    D Normal social life would be difficult without it

10 There is a small minority of people who

    A cannot distinguish between people's faces

    B are quite unable to identify people

    C have lost their earlier ability to identify people

    D lack the ability to know who people are from their appearance

Second passage

I am afraid I cannot convey the peculiar sensations of time-travelling. They are excessively unpleasant. There is a feeling exactly like that one has upon a switchback—of a helpless headlong motion. I felt the same horrible anticipa-

tion, too, of an imminent smash. As I put on pace, night followed day like the
5 flapping of a black wing. The dim suggestion of the laboratory seemed
presently to fall away from me, and I saw the sun hopping swiftly across the
sky, leaping it every minute and every minute marking a day. I supposed the
laboratory had been destroyed, and I had come into the open air. I had a dim
impression of scaffolding, but I was already going too fast to be conscious of
10 any moving things. The slowest snail that ever crawled dashed by too fast for
me. The twinkling succession of darkness and light was excessively painful to
the eye. Then, in the intermittent darkness, I saw the moon spinning swiftly
through her quarters from new to full, and had a faint glimpse of the circling
stars. Presently, as I went on, still gaining velocity, the palpitation of night
15 and day merged into continuous greyness; the sky took on a wonderful
deepness of blue, a splendid luminous colour like that of early twilight; the
jerking sun became a streak of fire, a brilliant arch in space, the moon a
fainter fluctuating band; and I could see nothing of the stars, save now and
then a brighter circle flickering in the blue.
20   The landscape was misty and vague. I was still on the hillside upon which
this house now stands, and the shoulder rose above me grey and dim. I saw
trees growing and changing like puffs of vapour, now brown, now green: they
grew, spread, shivered, and passed away. I saw huge buildings rise up faint
and fair, and pass like dreams. The whole surface of the earth seemed
25 changed—melting and flowing under my eyes. The little hands upon the dials
that registered my speed raced round faster and faster. Presently I noticed
that the sun-belt swayed up and down, from solstice to solstice, in a minute or
less, and that, consequently, my pace was over a year a minute and minute by
minute the white snow flashed across the world, and vanished, and was
30 followed by the bright, brief green of spring.
    The unpleasant sensations of the start were less poignant now. They
merged at last into a kind of hysterical exhilaration. I remarked, indeed, a
clumsy swaying of the machine, for which I was unable to account. But my
mind was too confused to attend to it, so with a kind of madness growing
35 upon me, I flung myself into futurity. At first I scarce thought of stopping,
scarce thought of anything but these new sensations. But presently a fresh
series of impressions grew up in my mind—a certain curiosity and therewith
a certain dread—until at last they took complete possession of me. What
strange developments of humanity, what wonderful advances upon our
40 rudimentary civilisation, I thought, might appear when I came to look nearly
into the dim elusive world that raced and fluctuated before my eyes. I saw
great and splendid architecture about me, more massive than any buildings of
our own time, and yet, as it seemed, built of glimmer and mist. I saw a richer
green flow up the hillside, and remain there without any wintry intermission.
45 Even through the veil of my confusion the earth seemed very fair. And so my
mind came round to the business of stopping.

1 One reason why the traveller did not enjoy the early part of his journey

176

through time was that

A   he was being shaken up very considerably
B   there was constant danger of an accident
C   he felt as if he had no control over the rapid movement
D   he was powerless to stop the machine

2   The laboratory seemed to fall away from him because

A   he had left it behind when he started on his journey
B   it had passed out of existence as he travelled ahead
C   it had disintegrated because of the violent motion
D   he was travelling too fast to see it

3   The slowest snail that ever crawled dashed by too fast for him because

A   his vision was blurred by the effects of rapid motion
B   any kind of physical movement was now happening too fast to see
C   he was now travelling too fast to be aware of small objects
D   a snail's movement would have been too slow to keep up with him

4   What impression did he get of the moon?

A   It was rotating and changing as it did so
B   It appeared to be either new or full
C   As he moved through time, the moon twisted through space
D   The changes in the appearance of the moon were enormously accelerated

5   Why did the sun appear like a brilliant arch?

A   It was moving so fast that it seemed continuous
B   The rapid passage of time made its apparent course seem continuous
C   The sun was circulating so rapidly that it was seen as a continuous band
D   This was the effect of viewing the sun's course from space

6   The changes he noticed in the trees were caused by

A   the varying types of trees that grew in different periods of time
B   changing climatic conditions in successive ages
C   the vague glimpses he could get of the various tree species
D   alternating seasons and passing years

7   Later in the journey the unpleasant sensations of the start

A   were replaced by an intense enjoyment
B   were intensified by the swaying of the machine
C   made him lose all sense of proportion
D   caused some confusion as he lost his awareness of things

8   The swaying of the machine

A   had no apparent cause
B   was an illusion of his confused mind
C   was caused by his intense speed
D   resulted in his inability to control the machine

9 What effect did the swaying have on the Time Traveller?

   A It worried him
   B It added to his hysteria
   C It distracted his attention
   D He noticed it only vaguely

10 He had delayed stopping because

   A he had been afraid of doing so
   B he wanted to see the developments of the distant future
   C he was in a dreamlike state in which it was difficult to take action
   D he had been absorbed by the strange effects of his rapid movement

Paper 3. Use of English (3 hours)

Answer all questions

Section A

1 **Fill each of the numbered blanks in the passage with *one* suitable word.**

_____ (1) careful most of us are _____ (2) trying to make a good _____ (3) on our fellow human beings (with the possible _____ (4) regrettably of our own families)! _____ (5) we may leave home without even _____ (6) to say goodbye to our nearest and dearest, we _____ (7) our uncongenial neighbour with a hearty good morning if we chance to meet on the way to the bus or railway station.

Throughout the working day, we adjust our approach and responses to colleagues so automatically that we are hardly _____ (8) of doing so. _____ (9) irritable we feel, our wishes vary in format from the subservient boss-directed, 'I _____ (10) if you'd mind, sir, if I ...' to the snappish, '_____ (11) those letters ready by three o'clock, Miss Wren,' (to the less glamorous typist) with an occasional 'please' as an _____ (12). We have learned from experience that _____ (13) to control one's temper, at least partially, may _____ (14) to mutinous staff relations and _____ (15) own unpopularity.

Far be it from me to _____ (16) that there are plenty of people (you and I for _____ (17)) _____ (18) courtesy and thoughtfulness are the same for _____ (19). But it must be admitted that as a general _____ (20) we (that is to say other people, not ourselves) may have a sliding scale of courtesy and charm, only too often automatically adjusted to the company we happen to be in.

2 **Finish each of the following sentences in such a way that it means exactly the same as the sentence printed before it.**
Example: 'I have no idea what the time is' she said to me.
           She told me that . . . .
Answer: She told me that she had no idea what the time was.

1 Although there may be a bad storm later in the day, the fishing boats are all leaving the harbour.
In spite of . . . .

2 They will have completed the redecorating by next week and then we can use the rooms again immediately.
We can use the rooms again as . . . .

3 He is determined to buy the house, whatever the price asked.
The price asked will make . . . .

4   She provided for all their probable needs.
     She provided them . . . .

5   If wages are increased too much, there will be further inflation.
     Too big . . . .

6   He behaved in such an extraordinary way that I wondered whether he was
     quite sane.
     So . . . .

7   I intend to take the day off tomorrow, whatever my boss's opinion.
     I intend to take the day off tomorrow, whether . . . .

8   To what extent does climate affect the habits and behaviour of people?
     To what extent does climate have . . . .

9   Coffee prices are likely to go up next month.
     There is . . . .

10   The dog caught sight of the stranger sitting at a table and immediately
     started barking furiously.
     No sooner . . . .

3   **Fill each of the numbered blanks with *one* suitable word or phrase.**
    Example: I realised I was almost certain to be seasick, so rough
              . . . . .that day.
    Answer: was the sea.

1   I wrote the date of her birthday in my diary in case . . . .

2   Rose: 'I've learned almost nothing for Friday's exam.'
     Ruby: 'Well, tomorrow's a free day. You'd better spend . . . .

3   When I saw the enormous dog bounding towards me, my first impulse
     . . . .

4   She smiled at us but her eyes were red and a little wet. She seemed
     . . . .

5   I asked her to report his actual words so she told . . . .

6   Many years before, Mark had rescued Murray from drowning. And now
     Mark was in danger of being murdered by Murray, the man whose
     . . . .

7   I don't mind your coming home an hour or so later this evening but under no
     circumstances . . . . .midnight.

8   Helen: 'I rang your mother's doorbell twice yesterday but she didn't answer
     the door, though I'm sure she was at home.'
     Hilary: 'She's rather deaf, you know. She might . . . .'

9   I may be able to make myself understood in English but I'm still very far
     . . . .

4   **For each of the sentences below, write a new sentence as similar as possible in**

180

meaning to the original sentence, but using the word given in capital letters.

Example: That child is always asking questions
　　　　　NEVER

Answer: That child never stops asking questions

1　Conditions in factories gradually got better.
　IMPROVEMENT

2　The trade deficit this month is higher than even the Government expected.
　EXCEEDED

3　His inability to control his temper has made him many enemies.
　FACT

4　I don't very much like that colour.
　APPEAL

5　His long absence has affected the standard of his work less than was feared.
　EFFECT

6　Yesterday the party had an unusually long discussion of election strategies.
　DISCUSSING

7　I suddenly felt very strongly tht something terrible was going to happen.
　CONVICTION

8　It is obvious that you have done him a lot of good.
　INFLUENCE

9　His mother was about to call the police when he crept through the back door, dirty and starving hungry.
　POINT

10　All but three or four of these sentences have been easy to deal with.
　EXCEPTION

Section B

5　**Read the following passage and then answer the questions which follow it.**

It would be hard to find a couple with fewer illusions about each other than a careers officer and a school-leaver with no qualifications. 'Ah,' says the careers officer, with no real hope, 'you look like a chap who wants to be a plumber.' And the chap who looks as if he wants to be a plumber stares back
5　with all the enthusiasm of a square peg who recognises a round hole when he sees one. The careers officer represents a large growth industry devoted to the fitting of pegs into holes and at the last count, he was faced with the nationwide problem of 48,178 pegs with no holes to go to. A combination of post-war population boom with economic recession has produced a youth
10　employment situation in which school-leavers, careers guidance experts and potential employers conduct a formal, sometimes sombre game of musical chairs. When the music stops, the school-leavers are the ones with nowhere to sit.

181

Unless they are naturally bright and academic they often see no logical or
15 visible reason why school is relevant in the outside world, and they may well
see, from their friends and families, that qualifications don't always get you a
better job.

'The sooner you're out and looking, the better,' said a 16-year-old from
Surrey. 'My pal waited. He got another exam but he couldn't get a job. The
20 girls in our year, if they got out early they got a job in an office or something,
but if they stayed on, they found they could only get jobs in shops and that. I
wouldn't stay for the sixth form, because the job situation doesn't get any
better.'

The outside world begins creeping into the schools when the children reach
25 the age of 13 and older, the age when they begin to make subject choices and
when, according to a careers officer 'they know if they're a scientific bloke or
more inclined to the arts'. The difficult part is bringing the outside world to life
with all its opportunities and realities. Schools are handicapped because they
are staffed by people who only know about schools. Careers services are
30 heavily influenced by what is readily available in the area, which may be
sausage-making in Wiltshire or ship-building in Clydeside. Somewhere out in
the world there are snail geneticists and landscape gardeners and girls who
polish Elizabeth Taylor's diamonds, but the careers officer knows little of
them. What he knows about is engineering and hairdressing and opportunities
35 in the Army. It is not surprising that this constant friction between
astronomical aspirations and uninspired reality produces cynicism in both
parties.

Wherever they work, sixteen and seventeen-year-olds can find themselves
used as cheap labour, picking things up off floors, fetching and carrying. £20
40 a week is good for a 16-year-old but it's quite possible to be paid as little as £2
or £3. That's in the living-in jobs like hotel work, or among the racing fraternity where trainee jockeys and grooms work for glamour and 'peanuts.'
There's a small breakthrough of girls into traditionally male preserves like
agriculture, but that may be because very few boys now would put up with
45 the low wages. Most girls, despite women's liberation, head straight for hairdressing, nursing or office work and dream of being swept off their feet by the
boss.

1 Why do the careers officer and an unqualified school-leaver have very few
illusions about each other? . . . .

2 What effect has the combination of post-war population boom and economic
recession had? . . . .

3 The careers officer speaks 'with no real hope' (l. 3) because
. . . .

4 'A square peg who recognises a round hole when he sees one' (lines 5–6) knows
. . . .

5 'The fitting of pegs into holes' mentioned in lines 6–7 refers to . . . .

6 What is suggested in the passage about how to play musical chairs?
. . . .

7 The realisation that 'qualifications don't always get you a better job' (lines 16–17) is likely to make older pupils decide . . . .

8 What is the connection between the experiences described in the third paragraph and the school leavers' realisations referred to in the second?
. . . .

9 By the words 'and that' (l. 21) the speaker means . . . .

10 In what sense does the outside world begin 'creeping into schools' (l. 24) when children first make subject choices? . . . .

11 'bringing the outside world to life with all its opportunities and realities' (lines 27–28) involves . . . .

12 The result of the present staffing arrangements in schools is that
. . . .

13 The fact that the rare occupations mentioned in lines 31–33 are 'some-where out in the world' emphasises the fact that . . . .

14 The 'astronomical aspirations' referred to in line 36 are . . . .

15 Trainee jockeys and grooms are willing to work for 'peanuts' (line 42) because
. . . .

16 Express in about 100 words the problems facing many careers officers who have to try to find suitable occupations for unqualified school-leavers
. . . .

Section C

6 Tom's parents, Mr. and Mrs. Brown, who are living abroad at present, have written to Tom's class teacher to ask for a general report on their son's progress at school and, as he is now sixteen, advice on whether he should leave school the following summer and join them, or stay on and continue studying. In the latter case, Tom would start to specialise in Arts subjects (Languages, History etc.), Science or possibly Music or Art. Tom himself has no definite opinions on the matter.

The class teacher refers to the recorded details of Tom's two most recent reports, which are shown below before preparing his recommendations. He then begins with a *brief* account of Tom's general progress, ability and attitude to study, makes one or two recommendations directly related to these and then gives advice about Tom's future course of action.

His report will consist of between 175 and 200 words. The opening statements are suggested below.

Name of Pupil: Thomas Brown		
Subjects	Form 4 (end-of-year)	Form 5 (half-year)
English	Has imagination but is careless	Some improvement but still careless
French	Speaks well but careless written work	Erratic—can be good
Mathematics	Very good	Very good
Chemistry	Practical work excellent	Excellent progress
Physics	Excellent progress A really keen pupil	Shows obvious interest and progress
Biology	Lacks concentration	Careless in detail
Geography	Satisfactory	Should work harder
History	Can do good work sometimes	Fair
Music	Shows little interest	No interest outside 'pop' music
Art	Fair	Lacks interest and ability

Thomas Brown is a member of the Fifth Form in Rigby School. The following report and recommendations are based on subject-teacher observations on his two most recent school reports ....

Paper 4. Listening comprehension (30 minutes)

(The passages on which the following questions are based are to be found in the Key to this book, which is published separately.)

Questions

You will hear each passage read twice over, and you will be given time to choose your answers to the five questions on each passage. Write the number of each question and after it the letter A, B, C or D for the answer you choose. *Give one answer only* to each question.

First passage

1 Brain surgery is suggested as an exception to most other things because

    A   it requires a certain amount of training and skill
    B   it is likely to remain a very expensive procedure
    C   having no experience of it, the writer has no definite opinion
    D   the services of an expert are indispensable

2 Packing involves the problem of

    A   planning to the last detail how the holiday will be organised
    B   providing for all possible needs in a limited space
    C   being firm with family demands to take superfluous objects
    D   finding enough containers to take everything required

3 Present-day camping

    A   demands a wider range of equipment and clothes
    B   involves more domestic chores than formerly
    C   is less enjoyable than it used to be
    D   is becoming more comfortable

4 The writer's description of cooking breakfast tells us that

    A   she has to stretch to reach the frying pan
    B   she is in a very restricted space
    C   she is kneeling down near the frying pan
    D   she is leaning against a shelf

5 What feelings does the writer have while on a camping holiday?

    A   She wonders whether she is really enjoying it
    B   She consoles herself with the thought that it is doing her good
    C   She is at least thankful to have a break from life in town
    D   She questions whether an outdoor holiday is as beneficial as supposed

Second passage

1   What is the writer's opinion of the value of the years spent at university?

   A   It is difficult to assess their value
   B   They can be extremely useful to intellectually-gifted people
   C   They can do harm to students without a suitable ability
   D   They may be valuable for intellectuals but not for other students

2   How does the writer assess the relationship between job suitability and university qualifications?

   A   A person with no degree may be a more capable worker in some fields
   B   There is no connection between the two
   C   A first-class graduate is always more suitable provided he is willing to continue learning
   D   High university qualifications are useful only in certain specialised jobs

3   The passage suggests that one of the shortcomings of a highly-qualified university graduate is that

   A   he may have very little practical experience
   B   he may resent having to take orders
   C   he may be too highly educated for his job
   D   he may lack sensitivity to the needs and feelings of his co-workers

4   Which of the following characteristics would many employers consider a disadvantage in an employee?

   A   Insufficient qualifications
   B   A high level of imagination
   C   A strong desire to get on
   D   Lack of practical sense and ability

5   In writing this passage the writer's main purpose was to

   A   warn students of the possible deficiencies of university education
   B   reassure the less academically talented person that he can be successful in his career
   C   survey the career opportunities for both academic and non-academic people
   D   recommend the creation of non-university courses for technicians

Third passage

1   What is a possible cause of exhaustion in a strange environment?

   A   Difficulties in adjustment to the new surroundings
   B   The very considerable strain of tackling unfamiliar tasks
   C   The effect of sensitivity to alien influences from the past
   D   The possible hostility of colleagues unwilling to accept a newcomer

2   The place assigned to the writer for his work was

    A   in a remote area

    B   part of the local broadcasting station

    C   near an army enclosure

    D   not easily accessible from the main urban area

3   Who had been responsible for arranging the papers?

    A   The writer's colleague

    B   The previous occupant of the office

    C   The person who was now in charge

    D   The writer's secretary

4   What was one effect of the dampness?

    A   The maps and the information sheets were all stained with rust

    B   The various informative papers could no longer be separated

    C   The envelopes were all stuck together

    D   The sheets providing information were covered with rust

5   What other irritation did the writer have to put up with?

    A   He was unable to keep his papers from flying about

    B   The fan made a constant fluttering noise

    C   He never remembered to secure his papers

    D   The movement of the papers in the draught made a continuous noise

Paper 5. Interview (12 minutes)

Section A: Photograph

1. *Suggested range of questions and topics.*

1 Describe in some detail the man reading.

2 What kind of person do you think he is: his circumstances, job, interests and personality.

3 Without necessarily being able to understand the French words, suggest from other indications the kind of newspaper this probably is and the kind of people who would read it.

4 What features of a very good photograph has this picture?

The kind of newspaper you prefer to read.

The relative value of television, radio and the newspaper in providing reliable and detailed information about world affairs.

Some of the problems faced by illiterate people.

Your favourite magazine.

189

2. *Suggested range of questions and topics.*

1 How would this fire engine get to the fire?

2 How can you tell that this photograph was taken a long time ago? (1875)

3 What are some of the improvements there have been in the fire service since then?

4 Suggest various reasons why many people might find this photograph amusing.

Some ways in which a fire can start in the home.

Some essential qualities a fireman must have.

Some of the jobs carried out by the ambulance service.

What would you do if you were in a large building—for example, a school or hotel—and noticed a very strong smell of burning?

A description of a very old family photograph.

Section B: Topic

Prepare yourself to speak for 2 minutes on *one* of the following topics. You may make notes on a separate piece of paper and refer to them during your talk, but you must not write out the complete talk and simply read it aloud.

1 Some reasons why there are still fewer women than men in the government or other positions of authority.
2 The value and drawbacks of having a pet (cat, dog, bird, hamster etc.) in your home. You can choose one particular animal or talk about keeping pets in general.
3 Your opinion of the value of formal examinations in assessing a person's ability.

Section C: Dialogue

1 Prepare yourself to read the part of MRS. BIRLING

Inspector:	Was it owing to your influence, as the most prominent member of the committee, that help was refused the girl?
MRS. BIRLING:	Possibly.
Inspector:	Was it or was it not your influence?
MRS. BIRLING:	Yes, it was. I didn't like her manner. She's impertinently made use of our name, though she pretended afterwards it just happened to be the first she thought of. She had to admit, after I began questioning her, that she had no claim to the name, that she wasn't married, and that the story she told at first—about a husband who'd deserted her—was quite false. It didn't take me long to get the truth—or some of the truth—out of her.
Inspector:	Why did she want help?
MRS. BIRLING:	You know very well why she wanted help.
Inspector:	No, I don't. I know why she *needed* help. But as I wasn't there, I don't know what she asked from your committee.
MRS. BIRLING:	I don't think we need discuss it.
Inspector:	You have no hope of *not* discussing it, Mrs. Birling.
MRS. BIRLING:	If you think you can bring any pressure to bear upon me, Inspector, you're quite mistaken. Unlike the other three, I did nothing I'm ashamed of or that won't bear investigation. The girl asked for assistance. We are asked to look carefully into the claims made upon us. I wasn't satisfied with this girl's claim—she seemed to me to be not a good case—and so I used my influence to have it refused. And in spite of what's happened to the girl since, I consider I did my duty. So if I prefer not to discuss it any further, you have no power to make me change my mind.

2 Prepare yourself to read the part of MADAME ARCATI

Charles: How do you know that Elvira was in any way responsible for Ruth's death?

MADAME ARCATI: Elvira . . . such a pretty name . . . it has a definite lilt to it, hasn't it? Elvira . . . El-vi-ra . . .

Charles: You haven't answered my question. How did you know?

MADAME ARCATI: It came to me last night, Mr. Condomine . . . it came to me in a blinding flash . . . I had just finished my Ovaltine and turned the light out when I suddenly started up in bed with a loud cry . . . 'Great Scott!' I said . . . 'I've got it!' . . . after that I began to put two and two together. At three in the morning . . . with my brain fairly seething . . . I went to work on my crystal for a little but it wasn't very satisfactory . . . cloudy, you know . . .

Charles: I would be very much obliged if you would keep any theories you have regarding my wife's death to yourself, Madame Arcati. . . .

MADAME ARCATI: My one desire is to help you. I feel I have been dreadfully remiss over the whole affair . . . not only remiss but untidy.

Charles: I am afraid there is nothing whatever to be done.

MADAME ARCATI: But there is . . . there is! I have found a formula . . . here it is! I copied it out of Edmondson's *Witchcraft and its Byways*.

Charles: What the hell are you talking about?

MADAME ARCATI: Pluck up your heart, Mr. Condomine . . . all is not lost!

Section D: Situations

1 An eighteen-year-old nephew or niece who has already been in trouble with the police for dangerous driving has asked to borrow your car while his or her own is being repaired. How do you reply to the request?

2 As an overworked businessman you can seldom spend an evening at home but you have promised that whatever happens you will take your wife out to dinner on her birthday. At the last minute this proves impossible. Telephone her and explain.

3 A five-year-old boy who is crying because he has lost his mother comes up to you in a busy shopping centre. What do you say to him?

4 You have seen an advertisement about an interesting job but obviously one line of the advertisement is missing. You telephone the relevant department of the newspaper to report this and to ask for the full text.

5 The members of your class have collected for a Christmas gift for your teacher. You have been chosen to present it and to say a few appropriate words.

6　You are seeing off an elderly relative who is travelling overnight by train. The relative discovers that the couchette reserved in a six-berth compartment is one of the two top ones. You try to persuade one of the occupants of a lower berth to change.

7　Although you normally have few difficulties with English, you find you cannot understand the dialect of the mechanic who is going to repair your car. Explain as tactfully as possible your difficulty in understanding him.

8　You have lost your temper with somebody and have said things you have since regretted. Apologise and try to explain your outburst.

9　As captain of a sports team you have to break the news to a very enthusiastic team member that he is going to be dropped from the team.

10　Your English teacher has written a word on the blackboard that you know is misspelt. Correct the teacher very tactfully.

11　A waiter hands you a bill for a meal you have just eaten. You check it and find a mistake. Explain this to him.

12　You have to book a person-to-person telephone call with reverse charges to someone in another country for a certain time later in the day. Make the necessary arrangements with the telephone operator.

13　A friend tells you that he or she has failed an important examination. What do you say?

14　You meet someone in a position of responsibility who clearly knows you; you have no recollection of him. How do you find out who he is without offending him?

Glossary

For reasons of space, only the rather less familiar words can be included here and the student will probably find it useful to have a good comprehensive English dictionary available when working through the various exercises.

The meanings shown are those that apply to the words as each is used in its particular context. Colloquial forms are labelled accordingly. Words are repeated only if in their later context they have a different meaning. Their arrangement in relation to the passage in which they appear rather than in alphabetical order is necessitated by the context-determined definition.

Where the meaning in context is an unusual one, this is indicated by the word *here* placed in brackets.

STAGE 1   Paper 1   Section B
Passage with model questions and answers. Pages 12–14
setting   surroundings, background
ribbed   marked with narrow raised stripes (like ribs in a body)
contour   level lines indicating equality of height
amble   walk slowly
corduroy   thick ribbed cotton material
generate   produce
sinister   suggesting possibilities of evil
silhouette   dark shape of person or object seen against a light background
mariner   sailor
make oneself scarce   disappear, usually to avoid trouble
boulder   very large stone
stride   length of step
mound   low hill
crenellations   spaces at top of castle defensive wall to shoot through
arrow-slits   small openings through which arrows are shot
hovel   small dirty house
insight   understanding of the inner nature of something
whiff   small quantity of air, usually with a slight smell
garlic   plant with strong-smelling root used in cooking
asset   advantageous quality or thing
render   (*here*) make
bray (n)   noise similar to that made by a donkey

First passage. Pages 15–16
roadster   bicycle, possibly in this case a heavy one
slant   rise or fall diagonally
flint   hard silica stone

tiptoe (v)   walk quietly on one's toes
nostril   opening in the nose
manure   animal fertiliser (for use on fields)
dip (n)   downward slope
assume an alarming significance   appear far more important and startling than it really is
exhilarated   feeling intense enjoyment
coast   ride without pedalling (usually downhill)
mudguard   metal cover to protect a bicycle wheel
incline   slope
dizzying   producing the feeling that one's head is spinning (turning repeatedly)
robin   red-fronted brown bird
cassock   long black garment worn by a clergyman
persistent   continuing, refusing to stop
stagger   walk with difficulty or unsteadily
cider   apple drink
take things to heart   react over-sensitively
impede   obstruct, get in the way, hinder
intoxicate   make us feel drunk with happiness
detour   indirect route
acknowledge   admit, realise
landmark   object clearly visible from a distance, used as a guide

Second passage. Pages 16–18

cavern   large cave
scan   look at carefully, look from one to another
barrier   (*here*) point in a station where tickets are examined
solicitor   lawyer who gives advice
punctilious   extremely careful and correct in behaviour
destination   place one is going to
disposal   putting into place
draped   covered with cloth (in this case, in stone)
nymph   Greek/Roman minor goddess; (*here*) statues
tranquil   peaceful, untroubled
loom   appear indistinctly, looking very large
benevolent   kindly, helpful, generous
ogre   cruel ugly giant
gainful   providing money
grime   dirt (often from soot and smoke)
awed   showing deep respect and fear
peevish   irritable
do away with   get rid of
into the bargain   in addition

Third passage. Pages 18–19

dolphin   sea creature, somewhat like a very small whale
shove   push forcibly, possibly roughly
tug   pull with an effort, sometimes repeatedly
friction   rubbing against
pebble   small stone
spasmodically   in irregular bursts of energy
strenuous   during which great efforts were made
greased   covered with slippery fat
tackle   get hold of and do whatever was necessary with it

196

flicker   show a very unsteady light, which sometimes almost disappears
muscle   part of the body that produces energy and movement
loop   the shape formed by doubling a rope to hold something
gulp   swallow to suppress sobbing
shady   somewhat sinister
kid oneself   (colloquial)   deceive oneself
impartial   not taking sides
tolerant   accepting other people's opinions without criticism
feebly   weakly
take off   start moving away
knot   a sea mile

Paper 2   Section B
First passage. Pages 26–28
barrier   a bar or other construction that prevents further progress
flurry   a small cloud of moving grains or powder
mean   average
ethereal   almost too light and delicate to form part of this world
gnome   an imaginary small bearded creature said to work hard underground
sleigh   a vehicle that slides over snow
feast (v)   enjoy a specially good meal
sheaf   bundle of corn
titbit   a specially nice bit of food
herring   a salt-water fish

Second passage. Pages 28–30
coronary   related to the heart
chronic   lasting a very long time or likely to happen again
bronchitis   disease involving lung inflammation and causing coughing
emphysema   another disease involving the lungs
determine   (*here*) influence
clinical   (*here*) concerned with medical specialist
doctor's practice   the number of patients that he treats
on a par with   on the same level as
premature   happening before it should normally
rebellious   refusing to accept authority
deteriorate   get worse
delinquent   in trouble with the law
precocious   developed before the normal age
onset   (*here*) decision to start
established   having become more or less permanent
prime   major, very great
Summerhill School   a well-known school whose pupils are allowed considerable freedom
corporal punishment   beating
banning   forbidding
beneficial   having a good and useful effect

Third passage. Pages 31–32
tradesman   shopkeeper or skilled worker
superficial   noticing only surface appearances
rural   of the countryside
conclude   (*here*) decide

flourish   do well, be successful
admittedly   it is true
contraction   reduction in amount
vigour   energy, power to continue existing
expand   get bigger
anonymous   without identity, unknown
substantial   of a considerable size
affluent   rich
hint   give a slight suggestion
fancy   a usually short-lived and unimportant desire
commodity   useful article bought or sold
enterprise   a business concern (or) willingness to do new things and take trouble
modest   without special importance
battalion   large organised body (of soldiers)
formidable   powerful and frightening
eruption   boiling over as in the case of a volcano
smouldering   suppressed slow burning
contempt   scorn, low opinion
trash   worthless stuff

Paper 3   Section B
Passage with model questions and answers. Pages 44—47
resort   place people travel to, particularly for holidays
at a premium   expensive because there is a demand for it
distinctly   definitely, certainly
itinerary   route
trailer   vehicle, possibly for sleeping in, drawn by another one
static site   place where caravans remain permanently
tow   pull, often by attaching to another vehicle
couple (v)   join two vehicles together for travelling
self-catering   providing meals for oneself
drab   dull, usually as a result of lacking colour
sordid   dirty and disgusting
image   impression people have of it
claustrophobic   causing a feeling of mental discomfort as a result of being enclosed in a
    small space

First passage. Pages 47—48
baffled   quite unable to understand
reveal   show what has been hidden
startling   unpleasantly surprising
imminent   likely to happen almost immediately
research   investigation
coincide with   be similar to
slaughter   large number of killings
exceed   be more than
fog-prone   likely to have fog often
speed trap   means of detecting motorists exceeding the speed limit
appreciably   noticeably, considerably
convoy   a group of vehicles (ships) travelling together for protection
frantically   desperately
hang on to   keep very close to for safety

Second passage. Pages 48–50

smash   break up into small pieces
crudely   without beauty, design or refinement; harshly, roughly
courting   considering marriage
usher in   suggest that someone or something will follow, bring into the mind
deprecating   *(here)* apologetic
sway   move from side to side (like trees in a wind)
diminish   get smaller in size
commiseration   pity
girder   metal support, often for the upper part of a bridge
cut me in on the spoils   give me a share in profits from a crime
secluded   isolated and not overlooked
quad   (quadrangle) school playground
Peter Pan   a boy in a well-known children's play who never grew up
dot   very small spot
conspiratorial   suggesting involvement in a plot

Third passage. Pages 50–52

the Depression   a period around 1930 of severe international economic difficulties
supplementary benefits   additional relief money paid in cases of need
caff   (slang) café
a pull-up   a place for drivers to stop
grim   extremely unpleasant
parish   area associated with a church; smallest area of government
tenements   block of flats, often old and dirty
terraced   joined in an unbroken line
urban   *(here)* living in a town
dole   unemployment relief money
casual labourer   person doing heavy work for periods when it is available
ragged   in old torn clothes
drift   wander without purpose
meagre   slight, insufficient
bug-ridden   with many insects in them
incubator   warm enclosure used for rearing new-born animals
swarm (v)   gather in large numbers (like insects)
National Health   *(here)* State provision for periods of illness
euphemism   word(s) used to soften an unpleasant idea
overawed   made to feel small and unimportant
cockney   Londoner, especially one who speaks a cockney dialect

Stage 2   Paper 1 Section B
Passage with model questions and answers. Pages 86–88

banish   force to leave (usually a country)
stroll   walk in a leisurely way
minefield   area in which explosives are hidden in the ground
nimble   able to move quickly
alert   keenly aware of what is happening and ready to take action
lethal   deadly
hazard   danger
propel   push forward
belligerent   aggressive
chariot   ancient horse-drawn battle vehicle

tank   armoured vehicle used in modern warfare
glare   angry fierce look
reprimand   stern criticism
resourceful   able to deal with unexpected situations effectively
fiend   devil
trolley   light metal cart used to carry shopping
ruthless   pitiless, very determined
prong   long pointed section of a fork
strategically   in a position where it will have the maximum effect
trip   cause a person to fall by putting something in his way
cripple   cause someone to lose the use of one or both legs
spike   a strong sharp point
amputate   cut off an arm or leg
formidable   powerful and terrifying
riot (v)   behave noisily and aggressively in a group
treacherous   (*here*) having hidden dangers
abound   are there in large numbers
lead   a strap for leading a dog
unwary   people who are not cautious and attentive enough
whine   cry in a high complaining way
groom   brush and make tidy
wield   use with the hands (often a weapon in war)
stab   a wound caused by forcing a sharp weapon into the body
hail   (*here*) an attack with a large number of small sharp objects
hurl   throw with force
soul   (*here*) person
tactics   planned methods for dealing with a situation
sou'wester   large waterproof hat
precinct   space enclosed by buildings
frisk   search quickly for illegally-carried objects

First passage. Pages 89–90

sheer   straight in a vertical line
crouch   sit on one's heels
crane   machine for lifting heavy weights
launch   usually a smaller boat used to go ashore from a larger one
in a jiffy   in a very short time
haul   pull with an effort
skipper   captain
jagged   with a rough uneven outline
dangle   hang loosely
fragile   weak
hawser   thick steel rope used in ships
clank   hollow metallic noise
mute   silent, speechless
anguish   suffering
relish   enjoy the thought of
sling (v)   hang from
frail   weak
octogenarian   eighty-year-old
disgruntled   bad-tempered
fanatical   having an exaggerated interest in one subject only; intense
shot   film photograph

withering   scornful, causing feelings of helplessness
screech   loud high unpleasant cry
cling   hold on with difficulty
mesh   network
callously   without sympathy, cruelly
peer   look with difficulty
infernal   hellish
presumably   (*here*) probably, what is to be expected

Second passage. Pages 90–92
buffet   refreshment place
swerve   change direction
impact   collision, meeting with force
dismay   anxiety, concern, possibly slight fear
desolation   emptiness and complete absence of comfort
converge   come together
accentuate   emphasise
dazed   confused and bewildered
permanent way   railway track
piercing   penetrating, cutting
predecessor   someone who has experienced the same thing before
buggy   light two-wheeled horse-drawn carriage
rusticated   countrified
apex   pointed top
ramp   sloping way or path connecting two levels
defined   (*here*) indicated by outline
shrine   holy place
gilded   covered with thin gold
escort   conduct with honour and respect
deity   god

Third passage. Pages 92–93
buoyant   optimistic, cheerful
dispel   cause to disappear
bog   wet soft ground
ally   supporter
target   an object to direct his anger against
lobby   hall of a hotel
aides-de-camp   officers assisting a general
comport oneself   behave
stately   dignified and impressive
literally   with the words having their exact meaning
suppress   force down under control
unparalleled   unequalled
outrage   shameful or shocking action or state of affairs
venomous   poisonous (as of a snake)
articulation   way of speaking, often with careful distinctness
woe   deep sorrow (old-fashioned)
artful   cunning, clever, (possibly here: with some dramatic art also)
devastation   complete destruction
sensibilities   delicate feelings
numbed   deadened, having lost all feeling
den   animal's home (also of thieves)

cater for   provide for as hotel guests
gangsters and mobsters   criminals belonging to organised groups
brigand   (normally) bandit, robber who attacks travellers
affected   unnatural, false-sounding
outright   utter, positive
wanton   deliberate and purposeless
gore   blood
grossly   in an enormously unsatisfactory way
litany   form of prayer involving the repetition of certain responses
pale (v)   (of the face) go white

Paper 2   Section B
First passage. Pages 97–100

discard   get rid of, give up
defect   fault
blemish   something that spoils, ugly unsatisfactory feature
tumble   fall
scrupulously   conscientiously, with careful correctness
emerge   come out
rookery   colony of rooks (black crow-like birds)
at a loss   puzzled, unable to understand
plumbing   pipes and other means of carrying domestic water
gurgle   noise of water running through a narrow outlet
sentient   having feelings
malign   having evil and harmful intentions
caper   example of foolish behaviour
attach   make even more fond of
shrubbery   garden of small bushlike plants
gasp   have difficulty in drawing in air
catacomb   underground burial passage
the weather held   the weather continued fine
drink in   observe with close attention and enjoyment
twinkle   shine irregularly like stars
shimmer   shine softly like silk
maltreated   badly treated
chuckle   quiet laugh expressing enjoyment
to-do   fuss and trouble (colloquial)
blissful   perfectly happy

Second passage. Pages 100–102

at sea   puzzled
wing   section of a house extending at the side of the central building
annex(e)   additional building, usually separate
untenanted   unoccupied
irrationality   illogical behaviour, inconsistency
flanked   having on either side
valid   acceptable, reasonable
baize   coarse felt-like material covering doors, tables etc.
of its own accord   without assistance
confront   meet, face
disconcerting   surprising in a worrying or disturbing way
vulnerable   easily hurt, damaged or destroyed
fortress   strongly-defended building

restrained   kept carefully within certain limits, without exaggeration
inappropriate   unsuitable
in the light of   when considered with the knowledge gained from something else
pedestal   a base on which something (usually artistic) stands
opulence   wealth, luxury
giddiness   sick spinning sensation that may make a person unsteady

Third passage. Pages 102–105
hence,   so, therefore
dwell on   speak about something for a long time
responsiveness   (*here*) showing what is drawn on it to the best advantage
overwhelm   (*here*) give far too much
shade   (*here*) degree of meaning
peat   vegetable matter dug from the ground and used as fuel
primal   (*here*) of the first days of the world's creation
toil   hard work
in an off-hand way   without showing much apparent interest
downs   the grass-covered hills of Southern England
swell   area shaped like a huge wave
turf   (*here*) ground covered with grass
sketch   draw
seraphim   angels of the highest rank
crimson   deep rich red (as of a rose)
sacred   holy
monstrous   huge and horrible
slouch   walk lazily and heavily
quadruped   four-legged animal
crayon   coloured pencil

Paper 3   Section B
First passage. Pages 111–113
splint   strip of rigid material for holding a broken bone together
sling (n)   strip of material for supporting an injured arm
at the mercy of   (*here*) dependent on
tiresomeness   unreasonable behaviour that annoys others
shawl   a cloth worn over the shoulders often for warmth
infirm   weak, often because of old age
humiliate   lower the dignity of
paw   handle (a person) unneccessarily or impolitely
contemporary   a person of the same generation as oneself
make up for   take the place of

Second passage. Pages 113–114
fringe   edge, border
cosy   pleasantly comfortable
densely   thickly
huddle   keep close together for warmth or protection
sprawl   spread over a wider area than necessary
stockbroker belt   an area of countryside in the neighbourhood of London where stockbrokers, who arrange the buying of stocks and shares, together with other well-paid businessmen, can live in comfortable homes
equivalent   corresponding area

fusion   mixture caused by running two or more things into one another
obliterate   cause to disappear
intrude   force one's way in
breed   produce
effete   weak, with no endurance
immaculately   perfectly, without a fault
subscription   money paid for membership
rate with   equal
links   area where golf is played
village green   area of land in a village used for local activities
prevailing   most common or widely-accepted
vicarage   the home of the vicar, the priest in charge of the church

Third passage. Pages 115–116
unprejudiced   uninfluenced by personal feelings and opinions, objective
eventually   at a point in the future, sooner or later
submit   present (v) for consideration
cross-examination   questioning in court to check previous evidence given
hearsay evidence   facts gathered from an absent third person
give him a line on   give some information about the possible identity of
specific   particular
culprit   person guilty of wrongdoing
fraud   crime in which money is obtained by deception
unravel   sort out from confusion and disorder
confession   a statement of guilt
circumspect   cautious in behaviour with full awareness of possible dangers or mistakes
analogy   likeness in some respects
trite   far from new and therefore over-obvious
angler   fisherman with rod and line
bait   object used to attract and catch (fish)
induce   persuade

STAGE 3   First set   Paper 1   Section B
Passage with model questions and answers. Pages 137–139
laced   decorated with the lace formed by millions of stars
skein   a loop of wool, silk or cotton thread
phosphorescent   shining or gleaming with no apparent source of light
trance   state of induced unconsciousness
blast   sudden violent rush of air
intimation   suggestion, reminder from certain evidence
strain   overuse, put a lot of effort into doing
imperceptible   almost impossible to detect
kernel   inner part of a seed or nut
clinker   brick with its surface glazed by intense heat
throb   vibrate with a strong rhythmic beat
flare   sudden outburst of light
streamer   long coloured ribbon of paper or silk
vermilion   bright red
thyme   sweet-smelling plant used when dried as flavouring
splinter (v)   break into long, extremely thin pieces
sojourn   residence
hoarse   with a rough harsh voice
overlap   extend so far as partly to cover another section (as in coat edges)

wade   walk in water
scratch   collected by chance from anywhere, of lower standards
craft   boats (here used collectively)
stern   back of a ship
pay out   let fall into the water by degrees
lustily   energetically, strongly
spray   clouds of tiny drops of water
tether   tie with a rope to something

First passage' Pages 139–141

scuttle   run quickly to escape danger
frankly   honestly and plainly
lore   facts believed about a subject
missile   object thrown or driven with great force
squash   crush
bear down on   approach with the intention of crushing
blare (v)   make a trumpet-like noise
for good measure   (*here*) in addition
guise   apparent form or appearance
bugler   player of a bugle, a small trumpet used in the army
troops   bodies of soldiers
hoot   make a noise with a car horn
resolutely   with determination
nip   move quickly
stint   task, job
juggernaut   huge long-distance lorry
rip out   tear out violently
engender   produce, cause
contend   express a firm opinion
abuse   misuse

Paper 2   Section B
First passage. Pages 145–148

virtually   in reality, despite a few exceptions
modest   moderate, slight
revarnish   provide with a new glossy coat
ritual   ceremony
veer   keep changing direction
maze   labyrinth, confusing network of paths
rutted   showing deep tracks left by wheels
plankways   boards along which wheelbarrows can be pushed
dump   heap of materials to be used in building
disoriented   not knowing how to find their way
stark   without any softening or decoration
clinical   with the cold bareness of a medical treatment room
window bay   projecting three-sided window
meticulously   with careful exactness
precariously   (*here*) with considerable difficulty
wobble   move unsteadily from side to side
trifle & blancmange   foods largely made with flavoured milk
lavish   generously large
equilibrium   (*here*) normality after overspending
snatch   short piece

gibberish   confused meaningless sound
flag   become less lively
trudge   heavy, weary way of walking

Second passage. Pages 148–150

submerged   under water
hatch   opening on the deck of a ship
focus   get a clearly defined sight of
skimpy   very short and incomplete
anodyne   soothing, undisturbing
erase   rub out, remove
unstable   unpredictable, unreliable, over-emotional
frailty   weakness
conspire   (*here*) work together
volatility   changeability, unpredictability, uncertainty
suffuse   spread over
antiseptic   medically clean and germ-free
denizen   inhabitant
inhale   breathe in

Paper 3   Section B   Pages 153–155

granted   accepting the fact that
source   (*here*) point from which information is gathered
conceal   hide by covering
depression   area of lower ground
crumble   fall into very small pieces
excavator   person digging out things
earthwork   defensive bank of earth (archaeology)
rampart   defensive structure of earth with a stone wall on top
barrow   hill covering ancient graves
blade   long narrow leaf
concentric   having the same centre
tramp   walk, possibly heavily
gravel   mixture of small stones and sand
shaft   vertical passage

Second Set   Paper 1   Section B   Pages 167–169

rampant   extremely common and aggressive
venue   (*here*) place
gratifying   pleasurable, rewarding
swindle   cheat (especially out of money)
bug   unpleasant germ (colloquial)
Welsh rarebit   melted and toasted cheese spread on toast

Paper 2   Section B
First passage. Pages 173–175

to his cost   to his disadvantage
the Lancet   well-known British medical journal
Identikit procedures   impression of a face created from various people's descriptions
competent   having the necessary ability
draughtsman   person who produces plans, detailed drawings of machine parts etc.
feat   achievement, act demanding skill

repulsiveness   appearance causing disgust
asymmetry   with little similarity between the proportions of the two sides
squint   condition in which the two eyes do not focus together
glossy weekly   weekly magazine (usually expensive) with smooth shiny cover
acquire   obtain from someone, not have as a natural or inborn ability
predominant   most influential, strongest, most important
entity   thing that exists independently
gait   manner of walking
ingenuity   cleverness in making use of circumstances

Second passage. Pages 175–178

convey   make known fully to the reader
switchback   construction at a fun fair on which small cars travel up and down steep slopes
headlong   falling head first
put on pace   increase speed
flap   move lightly to and fro, like a flag or bird's wing
scaffolding   wooden framework round a building in construction
intermittent   happening at intervals
palpitation   (*here*) rapid rhythmic vibration
merge   mix in such a way as to lose individual characteristics
jerk (v)   make sudden slight uncontrolled movements
fluctuate   move up and down, changing quickly and irregularly
solstices   twice-yearly times when the sun's apparent path is farthest from the equator
poignant   sharply painful
rudimentary   in its early stages
elusive   (*here*) difficult to gain knowledge of

Paper 3   Section B   Pages 181–183

peg   small piece of wood for fastening and holding things
boom   (*here*) a rise in numbers
recession   period of low economic growth
bloke   (colloquial) man
geneticist   expert in the science of breeding
landscape gardener   an expert in arranging gardens as if they were natural scenery
friction   conflict
aspirations   hopes, ambitions
cynicism   attitude of doubt and distrust of human motives
fraternity   brotherhood, people closely associated by their support of some idea
groom   person who feeds horses and keeps them in good condition
peanuts   (*here as slang*) very low wages
preserves   (*here*) areas restricted to certain types of people

Acknowledgements

The Publisher wishes to thank the following for permission to reproduce copyright material:

Phillimore & Co Ltd for an extract from G. K. Chesterton's *Tremendous Trifles* (102–3); Wm. Collins Sons & Co Ltd for an extract from Gerald Durrell's *Two in the Bush* (89–90); Eyre Methuen Ltd for an extract from Noel Coward's *Blithe Spirit* (193); 'Punch' for an extract from Lesley Garner's article in the issue of 9 March 1977 (181–2); William Heinemann and The Bodley Head for an extract from Graham Greene's *The Third Man* (48–50); Louis Heren for an article which appeared in 'The Listener' of 24 March 1977 (50–1); Victor Gollancz Ltd for an extract from Michael Innes' *The Mysterious Commission* (100–1); George Allen and Unwin (Publishers) Ltd for an extract from A. A. Jackson's *Semi-detached London* (145–146); The Hogarth Press for an extract from Laurie Lee's *A Rose in Winter* (137–39); André Deutsch Ltd for an extract from George Mikes' *How to be Inimitable* (167–68); B. T. Batsford Ltd for an extract from Barbara Øvestedal's *Norway* (27–27); A. D. Peters for an extract from J. B. Priestley's *An Inspector Calls* (192); Derek Robinson for an extract from his article in 'The Listener' of 5th September 1977; Peter Quince for an extract from his article *Country Life* in the 'Spectator' of 5 December 1970 (31); Hamish Hamilton Ltd for an extract from Terence Rattigan's *The Winslow Boy* (131–2); London Management for an extract from Peter Shaffer's *Five finger Exercise* (164); Severn House Publishers Ltd for extracts from Honor Tracy's *The Quiet End of the Evening* (97) and Leonard Woolley's *Digging up the Past* (153–4); Society of Authors for extracts from George Bernard Shaw's *Pygmalion* (165) and *The Doctor's Dilemma* (78–79); 'The Sunday Times' for articles by Judith Jackson and John Bell in the issue of 28 September 1975 (48) and Marie Fergus in the issue of 13 February 1977 (86); 'The Times' for an article which appeared 29 October 1962, an article by John Young, and an article by Charles Douglas Home which appeared 24 August 1971; The Times Educational Supplement for an article by Keith Horsfield in an issue in August 1977; Hodder & Stoughton Ltd for an extract from Mary Stewart's *This Rough Magic* (17); Dr William Thompson for an extract from his article in 'The Daily Telegraph' of 15 October 1974 (173–4); 'The Daily Telegraph' for articles by Hazel Leslie in 'The Sunday Telegraph' of 9 January 1977 (15–16). Clare Dover in 'The Daily Telegraph' of 24 March 1975 (139–40); The Estate of H. G. Wells and A. P. Watt Ltd for an extract from H. G. Wells' *The Time Machine* (175–76); John deLannoy (Agents) for an extract from Emlyn Williams' *The Corn is Green* (79–80) and Macmillan Co. Ltd,

London and Basingstoke for an extract from Sara Woods' *A Show of Violence* (16–17).

For photographs and illustrations:
Rex Features Ltd (69, 71, 73, 125, 127); Newton and the Gordon Fraser Gallery (129); Rex Features Ltd and A Devaney Inc (161); Carol Latimer (163); Rex Features Ltd and Peter Thomas (189); Pamlin Prints and C. R. Copeland (191).

We have been unable to trace the copyright holders of the following extracts but would like to thank them and the authors in anticipation of their permission: Articles by Robin Mead (44–45), A. V. Morton (90–91), Emma Lathen (126) and Anthony Maritenssen (2).

Figures in brackets indicate the pages on which the extracts and illustrations appear.